How to Market Your

Book
Free

The Essential Guide for Authors, Publishers, and Publicists

The Write Image

First published by The Write Image

ISBN 978-0-9860159-7-7

Printed in the United States of America

This book is printed on acid-free paper.

The Write Image

The Write Image
3255 Lawrenceville-Suwanee Rd.
Suite P250
Suwanee, GA 30024
info@thewriteimage.net
thewriteimage.net
facebook.com/howtomarketfree

DEDICATION

This book is dedicated to anyone who has ever dreamed of becoming a published author, but was too afraid, busy, intimidated, shy, confused, or uncertain to make it happen. May this book inspire you to take the first step towards your publishing dream.

Why Buy This Book

Whether you are a published author through a mainstream or traditional publishing house, or you are an independent published author, you are solely responsible for marketing your book. That is the plain and simple truth. Oh sure, your mainstream publisher will market your book for a period, but when that time expires you alone are responsible for how your book gets into the market place. Therefore, your earning potential is dependent upon you and your marketing efforts.

Marketing is one of the most neglected aspects of publishing, and self-publishing in particular. Many authors believe that if they write it, readers will come ... or in this case, buy. Marketing is **everything** you do to get the word out about your book, to gain a following, and to make sales. Marketing your book takes work, whether you self-publish or use a traditional publisher. Either way you have to let people know about your book. Marketing can be expensive, but it does not have to be. In fact, there are numerous strategies to market your book at no cost.

In this book, you will find 101 ways to market your book for high returns—**free**. This resource describes methods that offer visibility, exposure, outreach, and impact options. This book is designed as a resource to authors. The descriptions of the methods contained in Section Three reflect the information included on specified websites to ensure an accurate understanding of the benefits of each method.

How To Use This Book

The marketing ideas outlined in this book should be implemented within your marketing plan as needed and appropriate. The result of marketing is not always sales. Therefore, the outcomes of some methods in this book include results other than book sales. So keep an open mind. Place a high value on sales in addition to visibility and exposure. After all, when people know who you are, that your book exists, and what you stand for, they are likely to tell others, and thus, the snowball effect begins.

We recommend selecting five to 10 strategies in this book that support your overall marketing plan. Implement those strategies, measure the outcome, repeat if successful, adjust if needed, and then try a few more methods that make sense for you. If you find that some methods just do not fit your needs, or that you do not have the resources (time, knowledge, help, etc.) to implement them, move on and try something else. We believe there is something here to help every author be successful with book marketing strategies.

So choose your strategies well; give them time to flourish; and enjoy your publishing success!

Contents

Introduction

As authors, we believe writers have an opportunity to preserve their thoughts, experiences, and creativity in print, as well as in other forms of media. We all have a story to tell others. We want to share encouragement, inspiration, education, entertainment, and more. Writing is a way authors and readers connect. If a book's message is strong enough and is shared by many, it can create change.

For business people, a book is a way to share expertise. It is a format that potential clients can take home, study, read, and learn from. It can even be a way to prime clients before they embark on hiring you.

But a book—and the concepts, tips, experiences, and knowledge contained therein—cannot have the anticipated effect if potential readers do not know about it. This is where book marketing comes in.

There are hundreds of thousands of new book titles published each year, with self-published titles growing exponentially. In fact, the number of self-published books produced annually in the U.S. has nearly tripled, growing 287 percent since 2006, totaling more than 235,000 print and "e" titles, according to an October 2012 analysis of data from Bowker® Books In Print and Bowker® Identifier Services.

Bowker, the official U.S. agency that issues International Standard Book Numbers (ISBN), reports that: *2011's 148,424 self-published print books represented about 43 percent of that year's total traditional print output and contributed to the first significant expansion in print production since 2007. While print accounts for 63 percent of self-published books, e-books are gaining fast. E-book production in 2011 was 87,201, up 129 percent over 2010. Print grew 33 percent in the same period.*

With this kind of competition for the eyes and wallets of readers, how will they find out about all those books—including yours? How will they know which books address their needs and concerns, their goals, dreams, and hopes? How will they know where to buy those books, who the authors are, and what additional information the authors have to share? Readers will know about all of those books through marketing.

Regardless of how well written your book's content is, no matter how beautifully designed its front cover, despite the experts or celebrities who have shared reviews on the back cover, if your book is not marketed well it will not sell. Herein lays the challenge for authors, both seasoned and novice.

The question most often asked by newly published authors is, "My book is published: Now what?" The answer: Market, market, market to sell, sell, sell. Marketing is the means, not the goal; selling is the goal.

Imagine for a moment a still pond on a warm spring day with glitters of sunlight sparkling across its surface. That image represents society before the advent of the worldwide web (www). Now imagine a rock thrown into the still pond causing ripples to expand far beyond the initial splash, potentially becoming a wave. That image represents society after the advent of the worldwide web. For authors, publishers, and publicists, the "wave effect" presents new opportunities. Therefore, "ride the wave" and take advantage of the free-to-low-cost ways to market and promote published books.

Read on to discover some common, unique, and even unlikely methods to market your book—FREE!

P3 (Plan – Point – Process)

Marketing your book can be a daunting process, whether you went the print on demand (POD), e-book, or traditional route. Figuring out what works and what does not can take time, energy, and if you are not careful, a lot of money.

The Plan

A plan is essential in achieving your goals. Section one identifies important aspects of creating an effective book plan that will help you market your book effectively.

The Point

A strong thought-provoking message or key point is critical to marketing a book. In section two, your goal will be to develop the main point of your book and turn it into a message to encourage people to immediately buy your book.

The Process

In section three, you will find 101 free-to-low-cost ways to market your book. This is the process of implementing your plan and communicating your point. It is important to determine which methods in the process are best to reach the target market you identified in section one.

We have scoured many online and offline marketing methods to develop those contained in this book. Each method is an independent resource and the authors have received no compensation for inclusion here. The fact that a method appears in this book does not necessarily imply an endorsement. It is up to you to determine if a particular marketing method is a good fit for your book marketing plan.

THE PLAN

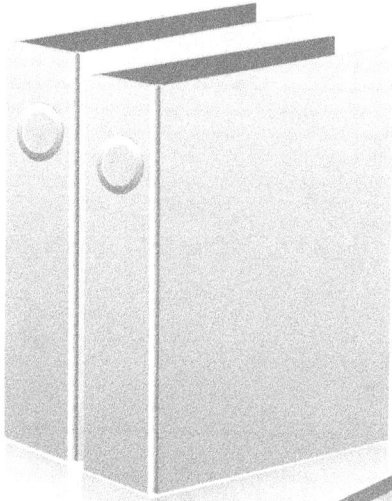
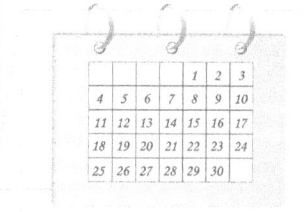
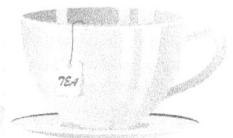

Developing Your Book Plan

Getting started with your book marketing project without the use of a plan is akin to setting out on a cross-country road trip with no navigation system, no idea of the distance you will travel, and no knowledge of how many miles per gallon your car gets, how often you should stop to rest, or when you should expect to arrive. Basically, you would be setting yourself up for disaster. Beginning with a plan is critical. Without knowing what you want to accomplish how can you know whether you have reached your goal? Your plan helps you develop realistic strategies and timelines and guides you in executing them with efficiency and excellence. Here are five important ways your book plan will help as you proceed through your marketing execution. Planning your book helps you:

1. **Avoid making up strategies as you go along.** With a plan in place at the beginning, you already know what to do first, next, and last ... and better yet, how to know whether any of your marketing activities are getting you closer to your goal.

2. **Resist the urge to react when new things crop up.** Inevitably, while marketing your book, you will have new ideas, exciting input from business partners and colleagues, or the desire to change/eliminate tactics that do not seem to be working. With a plan, you have a clear direction of what you wish to accomplish and how to get there so you do not have to entertain every idea presented to you. Of course, you should remain open to strategies that make obvious sense. However, this does not mean you should interrupt your plan to immediately explore each new option.

3. **Develop the foundational reason to keep going when you want to quit.** Your plan is the motivation you will need when times get tough and when it seems things are not working well. Refer to your plan often and remind yourself of your goals, strategies, measurements, and anticipated results.

4. **Know what your expected results should be.** One of the most important aspects of your book marketing plan is the results you wish to accomplish. Make sure they are realistic and measurable.

5. **Save time and money.** Starting with a plan and sticking with it will save you immeasurable time and money in the long run.

Here is where to begin with your book plan:

The Author

Determine your why. What is your purpose for writing this book? (To inspire, educate, make money, become famous, leverage for your business, career, or cause.)_____

_____

_____

THE PLAN

Goals. Goals must be SMART = Specific, Measurable, Achievable, Realistic, Time-focused. What are the TOP three goals for your book project? These should be quantifiable—how much, when, how often, how many. Example: Gain ten new clients within six months of the book launch.

1. _____
2. _____
3. _____

Define your motivation. What do you want to get out of the process? What does this book mean to/for you?_____
_____
_____
_____

Describe yourself as the authority/expert. Who are you, what do you know, and why should your readers care? What qualifies you to write this book?_____
_____
_____
_____

Describe the end result. In what ways do you expect your completed book to affect you?
_____
_____
_____
_____

Define success. How do you define success as it relates to your book project? What measurements will you use? (Book sales, fans/followers/connections/subscribers, revenue/income, new clients, average customer purchase, conversion of book purchase to client, etc.)
_____
_____
_____
_____
_____

The Book
Describe your book using the following elements:

Literary Type: (fiction, non-fiction, poetry) _____

Genre: (how-to, self-help, spiritual, memoir, autobiography, biography, romance, historical, mystery, urban, young adult, chick-lit, children's, etc.) _____
_____

Theme: (the main point): Answer the question, "So, what's your book about?" _____
_____
_____
_____
_____

Plot: (fiction): What happens throughout the entire book? _____
_____
_____
_____
_____

Tone: What is the tone of your book? (humorous, serious, contemplative, instructional, sad, angry, edgy, etc.) _____
_____
_____
_____
_____

Characters: Name and describe the MAIN characters and how they relate to the plot, even for non-fiction: _____
_____
_____
_____
_____

Narrator: (if any): What are the narrator's interest, position, and purpose in the book?
_____
_____
_____
_____
_____

Narrative form: (1st, 2nd or 3rd person) What narrative form are you using in your book? (use only one)

> **1st Person:** I noticed the way she viewed the magazine, and I wondered what she thought of it.

> **2nd Person:** If you wish to produce a quality magazine, you should follow these steps.

> **3rd Person:** She walked past the newsstand, paused for a moment, and then decided she would purchase the magazine.

THE PLAN

Title: If you do not already have a completed book, what ideas do you have for a title? List everything that comes to mind as a possible title, no matter how awkward it seems now.

_____

_____

_____

_____

Presentation: What ideas do you have for the presentation of your book? (cover design, book size, internal page layout, binding, etc.) _____

_____

_____

_____

Moral/Lesson/Knowledge Point/Takeaway for Readers: Name two or three main points your readers will take away after reading the book. _____

_____

_____

_____

Inspiration: What do you want your readers to think, feel, and do during and after reading your book? _____

_____

_____

_____

The Target Market

A target market is a group of customers to whom you decide to invest the majority of your marketing dollars, time, and efforts. A well-defined target market is an essential element of an effective marketing plan. When defining your target market, include a detailed description of as many of the following items pertinent to them. This will assist you in gaining an understanding of their interests, habits, behaviors, and influences to better determine how to reach them with the messages you will develop about your book:

Gender
Ethnicity
Age range
Education level
Occupation
Income
Marital status
Residence (rent, own, house, townhouse, apartment, condo)
Geography (region, state, city, urban, suburban, rural)
Family profile (children, grandchildren, parents in home, pets, etc.)
Lifestyle (hobbies, interests)
Values, religious/spiritual beliefs
Hobbies
Entertainment interests (music, movies/book genres, travel, sports, play or watch, etc.)
Sexual orientation
Health status/concerns
Social interests/concerns
Political interests/concerns
Favorite splurge (movies, clothing, jewelry, restaurants, books, music, etc.)

THE PLAN

Competitive Analysis

Competition is a contest for territory, a niche, or a location, for resources and goods, for prestige, recognition, awards, mates, status, or leadership. Competition is the opposite of cooperation. It arises whenever at least two or more parties strive for a goal which cannot be shared or which is desired individually but not in cooperation. Competition occurs naturally between organisms that co-exist in the same environment.

Except for those with whom you are co-authoring, all other authors writing on the same topic as yours are your competition. Therefore, you need to understand and learn their marketing strategies.

List three to five major competitors: (authors who write in the same genre or who target the same market), and describe how they compete with you. Do they have other products supporting their book? Do they have speaking platforms, businesses, radio shows, etc.?

AUTHOR NAME	BOOK TITLE	COMPETITIVE ASPECTS

Use the Competitive Analysis table on page 9 to compare your book with your two most important competitors.

1) In the first column, list additional key competitive factors.

2) In the second column, state how you compare to your competition in the minds of book buyers (Outshine Me, Equal, I Need Work).

3) In the third column, list the particular strengths that might help you position yourself against your competitors.

4) In the fourth column, list weaknesses or potential barriers to positioning yourself against your competitors (everyone has them). For example, being a first-time author could be viewed as a weakness.

5) In the fifth and sixth columns, state how your top two competitors compare to you (Outshine Them, Equal, Blow Me Away).

6) In the final column, estimate the importance of each competitive factor to the customer; 5=critical, 1=not very important.

Competitive Analysis *Insert Your Name Here* *Insert Competitor Names Here*

Factor		Strength	Weakness			Importance to Customer
Subject						
Price						
Cover						
Expertise						
Reputation						
Sales Method						
Accessibility to Purchase						

Write a short paragraph stating your competitive advantages and disadvantages.

Competitive Advantages

_____
_____
_____
_____
_____
_____
_____

Competitive Disadvantages

_____
_____
_____
_____
_____
_____
_____

THE PLAN

Market Research

Market research is important when establishing your marketing budget because you need to know the spending power of your target market. There are two kinds of market research: secondary and primary.

Secondary

Secondary research means using published information such as industry profiles, trade journals, newspapers, magazines, census data, and demographic profiles. This type of information is available in public libraries, industry associations, chambers of commerce, from vendors who sell to your industry, and from government agencies.

Primary

Primary research means gathering your own data. For example, you could survey people, use social media to identify competitor books, or conduct focus group interviews to learn more about your target market. When you choose a market research method or choose to employ a combination of both, you should be able to answer these questions:

What is the approximate size of your target market? _____
_____
_____
_____

What is the current demand within the target market? *(Understanding your target market and properly assessing the market demand for your book is very important. You need to know if your target market is likely to purchase your book.)* _____
_____
_____
_____

What trends exist within your target market? *(Book format preferences [electronic vs. print], pricing thresholds, growth or decline in number of books purchased annually, interest in various book genres, etc.)* _____
_____
_____
_____

What growth opportunities exist for you as the bookseller? *(Consulting services, DVDs, CDs, workshops, webinars, conferences, seminars, other products, etc.)* _____
_____
_____
_____

Budget and Revenue Generation Generation

How much you spend on the execution of your book marketing plan is based entirely on your budget. Unfortunately, many authors have no idea how much they have to spend on marketing or how much they expect to earn. Although the strategies and processes in this book are free to access and implement, you should expect to incur some expenses in the process of producing and marketing your book. Think of these expenses as investments. After all, you are investing in the success of your book project.

As with any other investment, you should expect a positive return on the investment you make in your book. Although income earned from books sales can be a good way to measure the success of your marketing efforts, there are many other ways to earn income or revenue related to your book. Therefore, you should expect to earn not only from the sale of your book, but also from related products and services you might sell as a result of being an author.

Here we review some expenses you might incur, or rather investments you might make in the production and marketing of your book. These are examples with estimated amounts inserted used only as a guide to illustrate how you can turn your expenses/investment into income/revenue.

ITEM	ESTIMATED EXPENSE/ INVESTMENT
Book production (coaching, editing, graphic design, ISBN, printing, etc.) for 200 books	$5,000
Website development	$2,000
Promotional items (bookmarks, posters, signage, postcards, etc.)	$ 250
Book fairs/festivals	$1,000
Ezine/Enewsletter	$ 250/yr
Photographer	$ 500
Marketing (10 processes/strategies from this book)	$ 0
TOTAL EXPENSES/INVESTMENT	**$9,000**

Now, consider some ways you can turn that investment into income/revenue through **book sales**.

BOOK SALE ACTIVITY	REVENUE
Book signings (fairs, festivals, bookstores): 50 books @$20 each	$1,000
Speaking engagements (back of the room sales): 40 books @$20 each	$ 800
Bookstore sales (gift shops, independent bookstores): 30 books @$20 each	$ 600
One-off sales (trunk of your car): 20 books @$20 each	$ 400
TOTAL BOOK SALES	**$2,800**

THE PLAN

Next, consider some other ways you can earn income/revenue related to your book, particularly if you own a **business** or have a **cause or special interest**. This is your **platform**.

BUSINESS ACTIVITY	REVENUE
Clients, customers (new people/groups who seek expert help): 10 @$1,000 each	$10,000
Information products (PDF, CD, DVD): 100 @$50 each	$ 5,000
Speaking engagements (your speaker fee; you're an expert): 5 x $500 each	$ 2,500
Workshop, webinar, teleseminar (teach solutions, results, tips, etc.): 60 ppl x $50 each	$ 3,000
Affiliate program (advocates earn to refer you): 10 referrals earn you $500 each	$ 5,000
Partnerships (with complimentary, noncompeting experts): 3 earn you $1,500 each	$ 4,500
TOTAL REVENUE FROM BUSINESS ACTIVITY (book related)	**$30,000**

You can see that your business activities can far outweigh book sales in generating revenue/income as a result of your book. Here is an analysis of your earnings.

Book Sales	+$ 2,800
Business Activity	+$30,000
Book Expenses	-$ 9,000
TOTAL EARNINGS	**$23,800**

This simple illustration gives you some items to consider when developing a budget and forecasting the earnings from your book.

One Page Book Marketing Plan

No matter how good your book is, your success is dependent upon effective marketing. There are many planning tools on the market today. The One Page Marketing Plan is different for several reasons. It will help you:

- Capture your ideas onto one sheet of paper
- Tap into both sides of your brain for greater achievement
- Create a tool to share with family, colleagues, employees, and investors

Sample One Page Marketing Plan

One-Page Marketing Plan for Authors

Author:	Nicole Smith		ISBN:	123-4-56-7890
Book Title:	How to Market Your Book for FREE		Distributors:	Ingram, Amazon.com, Barnes & Noble.com, Books in Print, NASCORP , Espresso Book Machine
Returnable:	X Yes ☐ No		Discount %:	55%
Book Description:	To provide 100 strategies on how to market a book with a budget of $0.00			
Mission/Objectives:	To provide authors with No Cost Ways to Market for a High Return			
Current Year Goals:	Win a Book Award			
What sets my book apart from the rest:	The book lists FREE marketing ideas where other books do not or they list very few			
Positioning Statement:	To be adopted as the MUST HAVE marketing book of the decade			
Offering to Customers:	Bonus: One Page Marketing Plan for Authors; Sales Forecasting; To Do List for Authors			
Sales Forecast:	100,000 books within 6 months			

Target Market	Promotion Strategy	Call to Action	Communication Method	Distribution/Fulfillment	Budget	Potential Earnings
Existing Authors	Reach New Markets	Attend Webinar; Buy Book	Email Campaign	Amazon.com	1,000.00	500.00
New Authors	Getting Started	Attend Webinar; Buy Book	Partner (Email)	Barnes & Noble.com	0.00	2,000.00
Girls Scouts of America	Mother Daughter Pearl Exchange	Attend Event; Buy Book; Sign Pledge; Spread the Word	Partner (Newsletter)	Author	200.00	500.00

THE PLAN

Author: Your name or the author(s) name

Book Title: Book title and subtitle for this marketing plan

Returnable: Is this book returnable? (i.e., can a book retailer return the book to the publisher if it does not sell?)

Book Description: Include a brief description of the book

Mission/Objectives: What is the primary goal of the book?

Current Year Goals: What are your goals for this year? What is the goal of your marketing efforts? What do you want to accomplish? Make goals specific and measureable *(See page 4 for SMART goals)*

What sets your book apart from the rest: How is your book unique?

Positioning Statement: What do you want people to say about you as the author or about the book?

Offering to Customers: Do you have a promotion for the book?

ISBN: What is the International Standard Book Number?

Distributors: Who distributes the book?

Discount %: What discount percentage do you offer booksellers? (Typically 20% to 55%)

Sales Forecast: How many books do you want to sell within a certain timeframe?

Target Market: Briefly mention the target market for your book including any important demographics *(See page 7 for instructions on defining your target market.)*

Promotion Strategy: A general overview of how you intend to promote your book. How will you build your brand?

Call to Action: How do you want people to respond to your marketing message? (Call, order online, schedule an appointment, register for your event, etc.)

Communication Method: What methods will you use to communicate your message? (See section three in this book.)

Distribution/Fulfillment: Will you sell through special in-store displays? What kinds of stores? Will you sell through a catalog, your own website, online through affiliates, or some other method?

Budget: Include your predetermined marketing budget so you know what you have to work with when planning your marketing tactics.

Potential Earnings: Estimate how much you think you will earn from book sales. *(See page 12 for an example for estimating revenue from book sales and other business activity related to your book.)*

Download the *One Page Marketing Plan* template FREE at: http://www.writeyourlife.net/ free-resources

One-Page Marketing Plan for Authors

Author:		ISBN:	
Book Title:		Distributors:	Ingram, Amazon.com, Barnes & Noble.com
Returnable:	Yes ☐ No ☐	Discount %:	
Book Description:			
Mission/Objectives:			
Current Year Goals:			
What sets my book apart from the rest:			
Positioning Statement:			
Offering to Customers:			
Sales Forecast:			

Target Market	Promotion Strategy	Call to Action	Communication Method	Distribution/Fulfillment	Budget	Potential Earnings

THE POINT

Message

A message is a key point—or several points—that communicates vital information about your book. This message should be consistent throughout your marketing campaign to help develop a solid brand and image of you and your book in the minds of your target market. There are several approaches to developing effective key points or messages, one of which is the STAR method.

The STAR (Situation, Task, Action, Result) method is used often during job interviews. This technique is a structured manner of asking and answering behavioral-based interview questions that have a higher degree of predicting future on-the-job performance than do traditional interview questions. Ideally, questions that are answered in the STAR method effectively get to the point of what should be communicated to demonstrate knowledge and experience about a particular subject or situation.

The elements of STAR are:

Situation:

The interviewer wants you to present a recent challenge and situation you encountered.

Task:

What did you need to achieve? The interviewer observes what you were trying to achieve from the situation.

Action:

What did you do? The interviewer looks for information on what you did, why you did it, and what were the alternatives.

Results:

What was the outcome of your actions? What did you achieve through your actions? Did you meet your objectives? What did you learn from the experience? Have you since used what you learned?

You can utilize the STAR method to develop a message to market your book. Developing your marketing message in this way will help potential buyers see themselves in the situation or challenge, understand the task or goal you want to achieve with your book, realize the action you took to solve the problem, and see the results you have achieved with your book.

Consider how many authors describe their book to potential buyers: "Hi, my name is _____ and I wrote a book titled "_____." This kind of introduction generally receives a lackluster response, if any response at all. To continue the conversation, the potential buyer might inquire further, but for the most part the author still may not connect with the potential book buyer. However, if the author tells the story behind the story, why s/he wrote the book, or the experiences that brought about the formation of the book, the potential buyer is more likely to be intrigued. People like reality, as demonstrated by the extreme popularity of reality television shows. They do not simply want to know the title of the book; they want to know what inspired the author to write it. Therefore, in a concise manner, the author's message should tell the story.

Here are examples of bad, indifferent, and good messages associated with one of Nicole Antoinette's books titled *Getting Beyond the Day ™ - Your Guide to Surviving a Job Layoff*:

The Bad

Getting Beyond the Day ™ - Your Guide to Surviving a Job Layoff by Nicole Antoinette is about how people can survive a job layoff.

The Indifferent

Getting Beyond the Day ™ - Your Guide to Surviving a Job Layoff is written with the millions of people who are unemployed or underemployed in mind. Each of the interactive chapters is filled with noteworthy suggestions to help readers plan for a stable life regardless of the country's economic state.

The Good

The fastest cars in the world go from zero to 60 mph in three seconds or less. As a passenger in that vehicle, you might feel anxious, out-of-control, even terrified. That is the most apropos illustration I can think of to describe the loss of a job. Within five seconds, you may go from employed to unemployed, leaving you nervous, confused, embarrassed, and at a loss for words. As a 20-year veteran of the information technology field, after experiencing that event a third time, my racecar engine sputtered and stalled. Without a plan to survive a job layoff, under the stress of financial pressures and self-doubts, I became depressed. I felt I had hit rock bottom, but as I thought about my situation, I knew things could get worse if I did not act. I became determined to find answers for my problems. However, I wanted to find them for others, as well. I began researching available resources and programs to figure out how to survive a job layoff. As a result, I authored *Getting Beyond the Day ™ - Your Guide to Surviving a Job Layoff* to provide people who are unemployed or underemployed with resources to help manage their careers, families, and life demands so regardless of the country's economic state they could develop a plan for a stable life.

In examining the hidden STAR in the "good" message above, here is what we find:

Situation

The fastest cars in the world go from zero to 60 mph in three seconds or less. As a passenger in that vehicle, you might feel anxious, out-of-control, even terrified. That is the most apropos illustration I can think of to describe the loss of a job. Within five seconds, you may go from employed to unemployed, leaving you nervous, confused, embarrassed, and at a loss for words. As a 20-year veteran of the information technology field, after experiencing that event a third time, my racecar engine sputtered and stalled.

Task

Without a plan to survive a job layoff, under the stress of financial pressures and self-doubts, I became depressed. I felt I had hit rock bottom, but as I thought about my situation, I knew things could get worse if I did not act. I became determined to find answers for my problems. However, I wanted to find them for others, as well.

Actions

I began researching available resources and programs to figure out how to survive a job layoff.

Results

As a result, I authored *Getting Beyond the Day* ™ - *Your Guide to Surviving a Job Layoff* to provide people who are unemployed or underemployed with resources to help manage their careers, families, and life demands so regardless of the country's economic state they could develop a plan for a stable life.

Here is another example of bad, indifferent, and good messages, this time associated with one of Anita Rochelle's books, a self-study course titled *Book Your Success: Write Your Book in 90 Days or Less*:

The Bad

Book Your Success: Write Your Book in 90 Days or Less is designed to help people write their book quickly.

The Indifferent

Many aspiring authors struggle to write a book because they lack the time and organizational skills to make it happen. *Book Your Success: Write Your Book in 90 Days or Less* helps would-be authors overcome these challenges and finally get their book done.

The Good

I speak to many audiences throughout the year about what it takes to write a quality book and the benefits of becoming a successful published author. Without a doubt, the two issues aspiring authors bring up most are: 1) "I don't have time to write a book. I'm a professional (or entrepreneur), I have a family, and other important activities that take up my time; where would I find the time to write the book I've been dreaming of writing?"; and 2) "I don't know how to organize all of the notes I've been writing on my computer and in my journal all these years to make it a compelling book." I believe everyone has a book in them, and that we all have the skill to turn our passion, knowledge, or experiences into a compelling book. As I examined the reasons many aspiring authors never get their book done, I sought to address those issues, all of which can be overcome with focus, commitment, and direction. So I created a simple system called *Book Your Success: Write Your Book in 90 Days or Less* to help professionals and entrepreneurs plan, organize, outline, and write a compelling book within the confines of their busy schedules.

THE POINT

Here, the hidden STAR in the "good" message above can be analyzed in this way:

Situation

I speak to many audiences throughout the year about what it takes to write a quality book and the benefits of becoming a successful published author. Without a doubt, the two issues aspiring authors bring up most are: 1) "I don't have time to write a book. I'm a professional (or entrepreneur), I have a family, and other important activities that take up my time; where would I find the time to write the book I've been dreaming of writing?"; and 2) "I don't know how to organize all of the notes I've been writing on my computer and in my journal all these years to make it a compelling book."

Task

I believe everyone has a book in them, and that we all have the skill to turn our passion, knowledge, or experiences into a compelling book.

Actions

As I examined the reasons many aspiring authors never get their book done, I sought to address those issues, all of which can be overcome with focus, commitment, and direction.

Results

So I created a simple, selfstudy system called *Book Your Success: Write Your Book in 90 Days or Less* to help professionals and entrepreneurs plan, organize, outline, and write a compelling book within the confines of their busy schedules.

Create a STAR for your book

Situation

Describe the situation you were in or the task you needed to accomplish that inspired you to write your book. You must describe a specific event or situation, not a generalized description of what you have done in the past. Be sure to give enough detail for the book buyer to understand. Give an example of a situation that resulted in the writing of your book.

_____

_____

_____

_____

_____

Task

What goal were you working toward when you decided to write your book? Describe the tasks involved in that situation. _____

_____

_____

_____

_____

Action

Describe the actions you took to address the situation with an appropriate amount of detail. Keep the focus on you. What specific steps did you take? _____

_____

_____

_____

_____

Result

Describe the outcome; what you received from the writing of the book and what a reader will get from the book. What happened? How did the event end? What did you accomplish? What did you learn? Make sure your answer contains multiple positive results. _____

_____

_____

_____

_____

Refine your message into a concise paragraph that can be read in 60 seconds or less:

_____

_____

_____

_____

_____

_____

_____

_____

_____

_____

_____

_____

_____

_____

_____

_____

_____

_____

THE PROCESS

A process or method of marketing creates brand experiences across many mediums to help you harness the competitive advantage of your book. It is considered a process because there might be several steps required to engage in, become familiar with, maximize, and see results using a particular marketing method. In this section, there are 101 free-to-low-cost ways to market your book. It is important to note that not every resource may be appropriate for you. For example, if your target audience does not listen to Internet radio, you should reconsider marketing through that medium.

Each process includes the following:

- Resource or method
- Description of the method
- Why you should consider using the method
- The source of the method (if other than the authors)

This book is designed as a resource to authors. The descriptions of the methods in this section reflect the information included on specified websites to ensure an accurate understanding of the benefits of each method.

• | • | • | • | •

1. 1ChapterFree

A book sales site, 1ChapterFree.com allows book buyers to sit in the comfort of their own homes and read a chapter of any featured book *before* they buy it. If they like it, they just click a link and the book is delivered directly to their door or desktop.

Why Authors Use 1ChapterFree.com

Showcase your book(s) to an audience that enjoys reading. This online book store allows you to list your book and a full chapter to help readers decide to purchase. You can include your author profile/bio, image of the book cover, and a description of your book.

Source: http://www.1chapterfree.com/

• | • | • | • | •

2. Affiliate Marketing

Affiliate marketing is an online advertising channel in which advertisers (online merchants that sell products or services) pay publishers (independent parties that promote the products or services of an advertiser on their website) only for results, such as a visitor making a purchase or filling out a form, rather than paying simply to reach a particular audience. Affiliate marketing is a "pay for performance" model, in essence the modern version of the "finder's fee" model, in which individuals who introduce new clients to a business are compensated. The difference in the case of affiliate marketing is that advertisers only pay their publishers when the new client introduction results in a sale or a lead, making it a low-risk, high-reward environment for both parties.

THE PROCESS

How Affiliate Marketing Works

Advertisers in an affiliate network populate their ad links in the interface, making them available for placement by publishers. Each link is assigned a commission, such as a fixed amount per lead or a percentage of a resulting sale on the advertiser's website. Publishers looking to monetize their traffic apply to join an advertiser's affiliate program. Upon acceptance to the advertiser's affiliate program, the publishers select and place the advertiser's links on their websites, in their email campaigns, or as part of search listings. When a consumer clicks on a publisher's link, a cookie is set on the visitor's browser that identifies the advertiser, the publisher, and the specific link and payment rates. When the visitor makes an actual purchase online or fills out a form, that transaction is tracked and recorded. Upon recording the transaction, the affiliate service provider (typically) handles all of the collection and processing required. This ensures fair and timely commission payment for the publisher and all the administration and verification necessary to guarantee quality sales and leads for the advertiser.

Why Authors Use Affiliate Marketing Programs

A primary goal for an author is to sell as many books as possible. To increase your target market with little effort and no cost, sign up as a publisher with an affiliate network. When you become a publisher, you allow others to market and sell your book to their customers. Thus, you have increased your target market without increasing your marketing budget.

Source: http://www.cj.com/

• | • | • | • | •

3. Alternative Retail Stores

Traditional or online bookstores are not the only option for book distribution, sales, and marketing. Consider gift shops, toy stores, wellness or fitness centers, senior centers, community centers, church bookstores, visitor centers, college bookstores, restaurants, travel stores, and other venues that make sense for the content and theme of your book.

Why Authors Use Alternative Retail Stores

When you consider your target audience or ideal reader for your book, you must consider their interests. There are stores that appeal to practically everyone, and those stores are where you want to market and sell your book. You may sell your books to these alternative retail stores at the wholesale price (usually 20% to 50% of the retail price), or offer your books on consignment, meaning that you provide a number of books at no cost to the store and, once the books are sold, the store pays you a percentage (usually 40% to 60%) of the sale price.

• | • | • | • | •

4. Amazon Author Central

Author Central is a free service provided by Amazon to allow authors to reach more readers, promote books, and help build a better Amazon bookstore. As an author with Amazon you are part of a special community. At Author Central, you have the opportunity to share the most up-to-date information about yourself and your work with your readers. You can view and edit your bibliography, add a photo and biography to your personal profile, upload missing book cover images, and use a blog to connect with readers. One example of how Amazon shares this information with customers can be seen in Author Pages. Amazon created Author Pages as a simple way for customers to more easily find their favorite authors and to discover new ones.

Why Authors Use Amazon Author Central

Author Central helps you to enroll your books in programs such as "Search Inside the Book" and "Kindle" so they are readily available for any customer to browse and buy. If your book is listed in the Amazon catalog, you are eligible to join Author Central. You can use your Amazon.com customer account to get started (or create a new one if needed).

Source: https://authorcentral.amazon.com/

• | • | • | • | • | • •

5. AmericanTowns

AmericanTowns.com is a local link to the people, issues, and activities that matter most in the lives of those who frequent the site. It is a virtual "town square," plugging visitors in to information and resources related to their city, town, and neighborhood. Each community can access tools to post local events, news and announcements, press releases, take donations, create a website, and more.

Why Authors Use AmericanTowns

AmericanTowns members can:

Post local events – AmericanTowns makes it simple to get the word out to your community. Even better, when you list on the AmericanTowns site your information automatically appears on your partner sites including Superpages.com.

Share news and views – The best part of a community is the involvement of the people who live there. So do your part by sharing your news, opinions, and events.

List a group or business – A listing on AmericanTowns makes it easy for others in your community to find your group, organization, or business.

Source: http://www.americantowns.com/

• | • | • | • | • •

6. Animoto

Turn your photos and videos into amazing marketing collateral. Animoto automatically produces beautifully orchestrated, completely unique video pieces from your photos, video clips, and music.

THE PROCESS

Why Authors Use Animoto

Readers connect with you over a message. Often, readers preview the back of a book cover to learn about the book which may or may not result in a sale. To reinforce the message of your book, you can create promotional videos about its message. You can also create videos to promote upcoming events, other products, training, and more.

Source: http://animoto.com/

• | • | • | • | •

7. AOL Lifestream

AOL Lifestream enables you to keep all your social network updates in one place.

Why Authors Use AOL Lifestream

It can be very time consuming to manage all your social media accounts. Utilizing AOL Lifestream or a similar management tool helps free up your time so you can use that free time for other marketing efforts.

AOL Lifestream members can:

- **Unite All Your Networks** – Get updates all in one place. Comment, like, and update your Facebook and Twitter, status right from AOL Lifestream.

- **Browse the Latest Trends** – Check out trends to see what everyone is talking about. Search and filter to see what's most important to you.

- **Follow Locations** – Follow your favorite places the same way you follow friends. Keep track of activities, comments, and photos for any location with Lifestream.

- **Discover and Share** – Update your status and link it to your location. Be the first to discover new places. Upload photos and let people know what's happening where you're hanging out.

Source: http://lifestream.aol.com/help/learnmore

• | • | • | • | •

8. Articles

As an author, it is important to demonstrate your knowledge and expertise in other forms besides your book. One way is to write articles to further illustrate your topic of interest. When you publish articles, you build a reputation as an expert. There are ways to be paid for writing and publishing articles, but this book does not focus on that aspect. To gain exposure as an author to promote your book, consider writing and publishing articles free. This will enable you to link the article back to you for a potential sale. Here are opportunities for you to submit articles for distribution:

- Newspapers

- Magazines
- Ezines
- Websites
- Social Media Sites
- Newsletters

Why Authors Write Articles

- **Exposure** – Reach your target market and be more accessible.

- **Connection** – Develop relationships so people get to know you better.

- **Reputation** – Show what you know by publishing articles and answering questions. Soon, you will be recognized as an expert.

- **Business** – When you show expertise, knowledge, and credibility, readers become clients and your business can flourish.

• | • | • | • | • | •

9. ArticlesBase

ArticlesBase is a free article directory where you can submit and find articles. You can publish your articles free or find content for your website, ezine, or newsletter.

Why Authors Use ArticlesBase.com:

- **Free advertising** – The author bio box is a tool to promote your website and personal brand that can be used to gain unlimited visitors to your website. People who read your articles will want to read more about the same topic about which you have written, so be sure to send them to more of your original content.

- **Viral marketing** – Really Simple Syndication (RSS) can be a gold mine. RSS feeds are so popular nowadays that you can gain an amazing amount of traffic. When you submit an article to a directory, that article can begin appearing on countless other websites. There are many high-visibility websites that can post your article, resulting in a flood of site visitors.

- **Boost your personal and business credibility** – Publishing your articles on ArticlesBase boosts your credibility and begins the trust cycle with your readership. Being listed with ArticlesBase is an excellent way to get started and build visibility, especially if you are hoping to be a published author.

- **Bring traffic to your site** – Distributing your articles allows anyone to read them. This gives you an opportunity to pick up more business.

- **Generate sales and leads without having a site** – Even if you do not own a website, having an article online can act as your website. Make sure you have completed your bio to let people know who you are. Also, include your email address so they can contact you.

THE PROCESS

- **Massive exposure to millions of ArticlesBase visitors** – Your articles can be read by the millions of visitors who view ArticlesBase every month.

- **Reach the unreachable** – Submit articles to ArticlesBase to reach customers you could not access before. The more quality articles you post, the more likely readers are to visit your website.

- **Build years of continuous traffic to your website** – ArticlesBase does not remove articles that have been submitted to its database, which means your posts can continue to bring traffic to your site for years to come. Articles may get picked up and reprinted years later.

Source: http://www.articlesbase.com/

• | • | • | • | •

10. Arto

On Arto.com you can share pictures, videos, create friend books, make a blog, and much more. You can participate in fun quizzes, interesting threads in the forum and join thousands of groups, or try some of the fun games.

Why Authors Use Arto

Depending on your target market, as an author, you may need to make yourself appear approachable and accessible to your target audience. Arto.com is a resource to humanize you and let your prospective readers know how much you are relatable.

Source: http://www.arto.com/

• | • | • | • | •

11. Author Exposure

Author Exposure is the place to get your debut and emerging books spotlighted, authors interviewed, books reviewed, and reader commentary all in one spot. Author Exposure is designed to bring the reader and the author together in a virtual environment.

Why Authors Use Author Exposure

With Author Exposure you can reach your target audience by creating an author platform, receiving book reviews, or participating in Book Radio.

Source: http://www.authorexposure.com

• | • | • | • | •

12. Author Readings

An author reading is an informal, free event where you read excerpts of your book to an audience.

Why Authors Use Author Readings

An author reading is an opportunity for you to showcase your talents as a writer. You can interact either with the audience at large (e.g., question and answer period) or with individual readers as they approach with a request for an autograph.

• | • | • | • | •

13. AuthorsDen

AuthorsDen is a forum designed to recreate the historical face-to-face author and reader relationship where authors create, share, interact with each other, and sell direct to their readers. This website brings that interaction online and throughout the world. AuthorsDen is a vibrant, free online literary community of authors and readers, visited by more than 1.4 million readers per month.

Why Authors Use AuthorsDen.com

At AuthorsDen.com you can reach readers by sharing your bio, books, blogs, events, stories, articles, newsletters, videos, and links to other websites. Readers can track and interact with you, and learn about your books and your platform.

Source: http://www.authorsden.com/

• | • | • | • | •

14. Auto Responders

An auto responder is a computer program that automatically answers emails received. Auto responders can be set up in your email account, through email marketing, on your online store, and elsewhere online. Auto responders are often used as email marketing tools to immediately provide information to prospective customers and then follow-up at preset time intervals. One great thing about an auto responder is that you can set up when the email will be sent, what will "trigger" the auto responder , and what the email will say. For example, any time you receive an order the customer can receive an email immediately even if you are not available. One downfall to auto-responders is that they can seem impersonal. However, you can overcome this by taking the time to write a personal note to your customers and use this as the auto responder email. You can even set the auto responder to send an automatic *Thank You* response.

Why Authors Use Auto Responders

Auto responders allow you to list upcoming events and offers, as well as respond immediately to book orders and inquiries to ensure no missed opportunities. This immediate response shows that you appreciate your website visitors, book buyers, and email contacts.

• | • | • | • | •

15. Bebo

Bebo is a popular social networking site. It is your life online, a social experience that helps you discover what is going on with your world and helps the world discover what is going on with you.

THE PROCESS

Why Authors Use Bebo
Bebo combines community, self-expression, and entertainment, enabling you to consume, create, discover, curate, and share digital content in new ways. The Lifestream platform allows you to receive updates from your other social media sites.

Source: http://www.bebo.com/

• | • | • | • | • | •

16. Blogs
A blog is a type of website or part of a website usually maintained by an individual with regular entries of commentary, descriptions of events, or other material such as graphics or videos. Many blogs provide commentary or news on a particular subject; others function as more personal online diaries. A typical blog combines text, images, and links to other blogs, web pages, or media related to its topic. The ability of readers to leave comments in an interactive format is an important part of many blogs.

Why Authors Use Blogs
Blogging allows you to share information about your book and your platform. You can share book excerpts, tips, awards, recognitions, highlights, and upcoming events. Blogging also allows you to be transparent by sharing your thoughts, knowledge, and insights with potential buyers and fans.

Some popular sites to create a blog include:

- Tumblr
- WordPress
- Blogger
- LiveJournal

Source: http://en.wikipedia.org/wiki/Blog

• | • | • | • | • | •

17. BlogTalkRadio
BlogTalkRadio is a provider of thousands of Internet talk radio shows. The streaming and archived shows are produced by anyone who wants to be an Internet radio host. Today, BlogTalkRadio is the largest, fastestgrowing social radio network on the Internet. A truly democratized medium, BlogTalkRadio has tens of thousands of hosts and millions of listeners tuning in and joining the conversation each month. Many businesses also utilize the platform as a tool to extend their brands and join conversations on the social web.

Why Authors Use BlogTalkRadio
BlogTalkRadio allows you to host a live, Internet talk radio show simply by using a telephone and a computer. BlogTalkRadio's unique technology and seamless integration with social networks

such as Facebook, Twitter, and Ning, empower you as a citizen broadcaster to create and share your original content, your voice, and your opinions in a public worldwide forum.

Source: http://www.blogtalkradio.com/

• | • | • | • | • | •

18. Blogger

Blogger.com is a blog creation site. Using the design templates, anyone can create a customizable, professional looking blog. The site features a variety of options to maximize a blog's presentation and usage, including photos, images, videos, mobile and group blogging, AdSense for monetization, and third party applications.

Why Authors Use Blogger

Blogger provides a simple way to share information about you, your business, your book, and other issues you care about. It could serve as a minibook site, allowing you to share excerpts, build a community around your book's characters, or provide tips included in your book. In essence, your Blogger.com site is a place to build an online community around your book.

Source: http://blogger.com

• | • | • | • | • | •

19. Book Awards

Through various organizations in the publishing and writing industries, recognition is awarded to outstanding books in various genres. To receive a book award, you must first complete an application and follow the submission guidelines for a particular awards contest. Submissions are typically judged by industry experts or other third-party judges. Some organizations charge a submission or reading fee to enter the awards contest.

Why Authors Submit Books for Book Awards

Book awards create credibility and visibility for your book. Winning such awards lets buyers know your book has been recognized as one of quality within the industry and among experts. Once you receive a book award you can update the cover of your book to display your award designation, send a press release to local organizations or journalists, post an announcement on your website, or host an event to celebrate.

For a list of book awards published by the American Library Association (ALA), visit http://www.ala.org/awardsgrants/awards/browse/bpma?showfilter=no

• | • | • | • | • | •

20. Book Clubs

A book club is a group of people who meet to discuss the books they read. Often, book club members recommend a particular book to the group. Each member purchases his/her own copy, reads it—sometimes independently, sometimes in the group—then the group discusses key points from the book.

THE PROCESS

Why Authors Participate in Book Clubs
Book clubs provide an ideal platform for you to gain exposure to a broad market and to sell multiple books. As an author, you can contact local book clubs and visit their meetings to engage in conversations about your book. To expand your exposure to book clubs you can become a *Virtual Author* where you participate over the Internet or by phone.

• | • | • | • | •

21. BookDaily
There are so many choices in today's fragmented literary world that it is harder than ever to discover good new authors and books. The purpose of BookDaily is to help readers find the authors that they will enjoy reading. BookDaily introduces authors to new readers by providing a sample chapter from the author's books.

Why Authors Use BookDaily
A free BookDaily author account allows you to:
- Post the first chapter of any of your books for reader review
- Post your biography and photo
- Include a link to your website or your blog for new traffic and SEO value
- Load video about your book
- Receive a regular author marketing newsletter from thought leaders in digital book marketing
- Promote your work with a free widget, press release information, and more
- Free Bonus: Receive a free copy of the ebook, "Online Marketing for Authors", loaded with online marketing information

Source: http://www.bookdaily.com/authorsignup

• | • | • | • | •

22. Book Reviews
A book review is a description, critical analysis, and evaluation of the quality, meaning, and significance of a book. Reviews should focus on the book's purpose, content, and authority. A critical book review is not a book report or summary. It is a reaction paper in which strengths and weaknesses of the material are analyzed. It includes a statement of what the author has tried to do and evaluates how well (in the opinion of the reviewer) the author has succeeded, presenting evidence to support this evaluation.

There are two ways to get exposure for your book:
- Reviewers write about your book
- You write about other books – including a byline that links to your book – on the following sites:
  - Barnes & Noble
  - Amazon.com

- Other book retail sites

Why Authors Obtain Book Reviews

Book reviews are similar to word-of-mouth advertising. These third-party reviews allow potential readers to obtain an unbiased perspective of your book to aid their book-buying process.

• | • | • | • | •

23. Book Signings

Book signing events are organized by authors or their supporters for the purpose of having the author sign books for those interested in buying. These events can be held at bookstores, festivals, conferences, or other events. The author is introduced, greets the audience, and may even read several excerpts from the book. It is customary for authors to take questions from the audience about the book or the process of writing.

Why Authors Use Book Signings

Book signings offer a great deal of exposure and visibility for you and your book. Readers enjoy meeting and interacting with authors and having a signed copy in their possession. Adding your signature to your book can increase its value.

• | • | • | • | •

24. Book Trailers

A book trailer is a brief video advertisement that employs techniques similar to those of movie trailers. They are circulated on television and online in most common digital video formats. Book trailers can be produced using author interviews, dramatic theme depictions, theme overviews, and others techniques.

Why Authors Use Book Trailers

A book trailer encourages potential buyers' emotional involvement in your book. It is a unique marketing method to describe your book. Book trailers can be posted online in various ways, including:

- Video sharing sites
- Websites
- Emails
- Blogs

In addition, book trailers can be used as your introduction in presentations to groups, for speaking engagements, at book festivals, on television, and in other ways.

• | • | • | • | •

25. BookBlogs

A social media site, BookBlogs.com connects authors with readers, reviewers, and other lovers of books. Anyone can create a profile page and include a bio, a list of authored books, links to

THE PROCESS

your book blog or website, and other unique information. You may join discussion forums and groups to build a following for your book.

Why Authors Use BookBlogs

Exposure to readers is what this social space is all about. The more active you are, the more visibility you gain, and the greater the opportunity for buyers to know about your book.

Source: *http://bookblogs.ning.com/*

• | • | • | • | •

26. BookBuzzr

BookBuzzr claims to be the world's number one provider of book marketing technologies for authors. The site offers both free and paid options – free technologies because if you like them you will tell other authors about them and paid options because more ambitious authors are willing to pay for premium marketing technologies (such as BookBuzzr Games). If you win, they win.

Why Authors Utilize BookBuzzr

Members can use the following free BookBuzzr technologies:

- **Book Widget** – An excellent replacement for your static book cover image. Just copy and paste a few lines of code onto your website or blog and you are good to go. No technical expertise necessary. Its pages flip like a real book. You can package additional information about yourself inside the widget. Potential book buyers can explore your book without leaving your main page. Your fans can also share your book on their websites, blogs, or Facebook profiles.

- **MiniWidget** – Go where the Book Widget does not go; for example, on your Wordpress. com blog or a narrow sidebar. Mini-widget is light, fast, and it flips pages like a real book. It is a perfect invitation to get your readers to sample your book.

- **BookTweeter** – Market and promote your book on Twitter. You can schedule auto tweets on Twitter in a way that does not irritate or annoy your followers. This provides a perfect tool to gain additional exposure on Twitter without wasting hours every day.

- **Email Signature** – Invite every one of your email recipients to sample the pages of your book. BookBuzzr Email Signature is the perfect way to differentiate yourself as an author in the emails you send out.

- **Search Optimized fReado Author and Book Listing** – Signing up for BookBuzzr gives you a free listing on fReado.com, the world's biggest book giveaway site. Since Google and other search engines index fReado, a listing and a link to your site on fReado will potentially raise the search engine ranking for your own site or blog.

- **Book Sampler** – Potential buyers learn more about you as they flip pages, previewing your book. You can add links to multiple websites where readers can buy your book. Your content will be indexed by search engines so readers can discover your book while they are searching online.

Sourc: http://www.bookbuzzr.com/

• | • | • | • | •

27. Bookfestivals

Bookfestivals.com is a JM Northern Media website founded in 1999 and produces entertainment and education events around the world, including DIY Convention: Do It Yourself in Film, Music & Books, Hollywood Book Festival, and New York Book Festival.

Why Authors Use Bookfestivals

On the Bookfestivals website you can add a listing for a book festival or author reading to its general database at no cost. Simply fill out the form and JM Northern Media will upload your information promptly to its website.

Source: http://bookfestivals.com

• | • | • | • | •

28. Bookhitch

Bookhitch offers publishers and authors both free and premium listings. Free listings include basic information, five key search words, a 60-word description, and a link where the book can be purchased. Paid listings include twice the description length, a book review, an author biography, a picture of your book, and priority over free listings in search queries. Visitors can search by title, author, ISBN, or genre to find books in their areas of interest. Simply clicking a link brings them in contact with the Publisher/Author for more information and purchase, eliminating the need for a middleman.

Why Authors Use Bookhitch.com

Bookhitch brings the author and reader together in a virtual community, providing access to your target market.

Source: http://www.bookhitch.com/

• | • | • | • | •

29. Bundling

As an author, bundling refers to combining a book with complementary products, services, or programs at a slightly discounted price to add perceived value for the buyer. Bundling gives buyers an incentive to purchase a complete package of products and services at a better price than purchasing the items individually.

Why Authors Use Bundling

THE PROCESS

Marketing bundled products allows you to reach a broader audience. Additional items sold along with your book could be products, services, or programs you offer, or those of others with whom you have an agreement.

• | • | • | • | • | •

30. Café Mom

Café Mom is an online community where thousands of moms come together every day to chat, share photos, and make friends.

Why Authors Use Café Mom

As a Café Mom member you can interact with an active and influential online community of moms, particularly useful if this demographic fits the target market for your book. Network with the community, join groups, give advice, voice your opinions, and share information about your book, your expertise, and your platform.

Source: http://www.cafemom.com

• | • | • | • | • | •

31. Charities

There are hundreds of thousands of nonprofit charities in the United States alone. Charities often seek creative ways to raise funds, to offer incentives to donors, or to thank board members, sponsors, and volunteers. Your book could be just the gift or incentive your favorite charity is looking for to help bolster its ongoing efforts.

Why Authors Use Charities

By offering your book to a charity you have a supportive, third-party marketing and promotions team that can help get your book into the hands of many who might not otherwise know about it. As charities exercise their outreach efforts, using your book as an incentive or gift could help increase visibility. Make a list of your favorite charities and ask if they would be interested in offering your book to their supporters. There are three ways to do this:

1) you can donate a specified number of books and allow the charity to distribute them as they wish, using the books as your in-kind donation;

2) you can sell the books to the charity for a highly discounted rate and allow them to distribute at their discretion; or

3) you can offer to host a fundraising drive to benefit the charity by offering a portion of the proceeds from book sales to the charity for a limited time. People enjoy knowing they are giving to a good cause and getting a great book in the process.

Sources: http://www.charitynavigator.org/

Sources: http://www.charities.org/learn

Sources: http://www.independentcharities.org/search/findset.asp?Title=View+Our+Natio nal+And+International+Members&c=n

• | • | • | • | •

32. Conference Calls

Conference calls are used most often in business as a convenient way to connect people in different locations. Each participant calls into a common phone number, enters a pass code or access code, and is connected to the conference call.

Why Authors Use Conference Calls

Conference calls provide a great resource for authors to get the word out about a book launch or other event, a promotion, or an author appearance, or to rally supporters to assist you in some way. Typically, participants are within your "inner circle"—supporters, employees, volunteers, commissioned sales persons, affiliate program members, joint venture partners, mastermind group participants, or others—who meet to strategize or offer suggestions for a mutually beneficial event or activity. Although the focus of the meeting might be your book or event, there should be a buy-in or benefit to other callers for participating (i.e. commission, visibility).

Source: http://www.freeconferencecall.com/

• | • | • | • | •

33. Constant Contact

Through its unique combination of online marketing tools and free personalized coaching, Constant Contact helps small businesses, associations, authors, and non-profits connect and engage with their audiences. Launched in 1998, Constant Contact has long championed the needs of small organizations, providing them with an easy way to create and build successful, lasting customer relationships. The support team at Constant Contact provides useful suggestions for maximizing the effectiveness of your email marketing campaigns.

Why Authors Use Constant Contact

Email marketing—or Engagement Marketing® as Constant Contact refers to it—is the act of sending valuable, opt-in messages to subscribers that help build visibility, customers, and supporters. Email marketing works best when done through a planned, consistent method. As an author, you can share excerpts of your book, information about your appearances, book signings and speaking engagements, discounts or launches of new books, products, or services, or offer subscribers the chance to purchase your book from your website.

Source: http://www.constantcontact.com

• | • | • | • | •

34. Contests

Everyone likes to win a prize. You could host a simple contest by posting a question on your website, blog, or social media site and offer your book as the prize for the first five or ten respondents with the correct answer. The respondents should enter their name and email address to enter the contest, thus providing you with this information for future contact. Contests should be free to enter and rules should explain exactly what the winner will receive, as well as advise entrants that they will be added to your subscribers list. Be sure to review rules and restrictions on social media sites for running contests. Some, such as Facebook, have strict rules prohibiting activities such as requiring contest entrants to "Like" your page to enter your contest.

Why Authors Use Contests
Hosting contests is a way for you to increase exposure for—and interest in—your book. Contests are also a great way to increase your subscriber list, social media followers, and business contacts. Add contacts you collect from contest entrants to your email marketing campaigns, book and event promotions, and other communications.

• | • | • | • | • | •

35. Craigslist
Craigslist in an online community featuring local classified ads and forums, where people sell a variety of goods and services. It is community moderated and largely free.

Why Authors Use Craigslist
On Craigslist you can create an ad for your book, perhaps offering a promotional price or bonus offer, product, or service to accompany your book. You can also start discussion forums, list services offered, and add upcoming events such as book signings and other appearances.

Source: http://www.craigslist.com

• | • | • | • | • | •

36. Delicious
Delicious is a social bookmarking service allowing you to save all your bookmarks online, share them with other people, and see what they are bookmarking. You can view the most popular bookmarks across many areas of interest. In addition, search and tagging tools help you keep track of your entire bookmark collection and find interesting new bookmarks from people like you.

Why Authors Use Delicious
Delicious allow authors to share bookmarks of websites that sell their books, articles, products, and services.

Source: http://www.delicious.com/

• | • | • | • | • | •

37. Digg
Digg is a place for people to discover and share content from anywhere on the web. From the

biggest online destinations to the most obscure blogs, Digg features the best sites as voted on by its users.

Why Authors Use Digg

Digg members can create a profile, publish content, and develop a following.

Source: http://digg.com

• | • | • | • | •

38. eHow

An online provider of video and article content in numerous websites, eHow offers you the opportunity to position yourself as an expert or to build your brand. Articles uploaded to eHow have a mini-bio of the author and could include your book title, website, and other information.

Why Authors Use eHow

Providing articles about your business or your book further positions you as an expert and offers valuable search engine optimization for your name and book title. Your articles should be specific to your area of specialization, particularly the content of your book. Include strategic keywords in your article posts and include a link to your website so viewers can purchase your book or learn more about you and your business.

Source: http://www.demandstudios.com/work-from-home.html

• | • | • | • | •

39. Elevator Speech

Elevator Speech is the phrase used to describe a brief introduction you might provide to an individual or group to whom you introduce yourself. It should be brief enough to present, theoretically, while riding on the elevator from one floor to the next and should include the most basic information about you to allow others to quickly and easily grasp your interests and expertise.

Why Authors Use an Elevator Speech

The elevator speech concept provides a concise way to share with others what your book is about and who you are. Although brief, it should give enough information for others to clearly understand your book's theme or your business platform yet intrigue the listener enough to encourage them to ask questions and learn more.

• | • | • | • | •

40. Email

Electronic mail, or email, is a method of exchanging digital messages. Email systems are based on a store-and-or-ward model in which computer server systems accept, forward, deliver, and store messages on behalf of users who only need to connect to the email infrastructure, typically an email server, with a network-enabled device (e.g., a personal computer) for the duration of message submission or retrieval. An electronic mail message consists of two components: the header, and the body—the email's content. The message header contains control information including the originator's email address and one or more recipient addresses. Usually additional information is added, such as a subject header field.

Why Authors Use Email

Using the following email features helps you sell your book quickly and easily:

- Signature
- Barter
- Forward
- Email Coupons
- Custom Background
- Thank You

Signature

The signature feature, typically added to the very end of your email message, is an important addition to every email you send. Even your friends may not always remember your website address or business phone number and will quickly look to an old email to retrieve your contact information.

Among your email options or settings should be an option that reads similar to this: *Show a signature on all outgoing messages.* This will enable you to create a standard message to market your book which automatically appears in each outgoing email without retyping the information each time. When preparing an email signature it is important to include your name, your book title, the ISBN, your website address, and a phone number. You may also want to consider these other features:

- Hyperlink – enables the receiver of the email to click on the hyperlink to navigate directly to the URL
- Picture – enables the receiver of the email to see a picture of your book
- Business Card – enables the receiver to save your contact information for future use

Here is a sample email signature:

Breakthrough is imminent,
Nicole Antoinette
Victory of the People, Beyond Praise!
Author of Your Guide to Surviving a Job Layoff http://amzn.to/VmDz4B
ISBN: 9780986015922
http://gettingbeyondtheday.com/

Barter

Consider finding several people who will allow you to include information about your book within their email signature. This is an easy way to spread the word about your book. Ask a colleague or friend if they will "swap" a line of their signature with you. You will add a line at the bottom of your signature with a link to whatever they are marketing and they will do the same.

Forward

The email forward feature is equivalent to a personal phone call to inform others of your book, but it is faster. Within your message you can request the recipient to forward your email to others.

Email Coupons

Coupons are a great email networking tool. Include a special coupon available only to those who receive your emails. If you have one, extend this to your newsletter. Offer a special coupon for anyone who signs up for your newsletter.

Custom Background

Creating a custom background for your email is easier to do than it sounds. If you use Microsoft Outlook or a similar program you can find directions at: http://office.microsoft.com/en-us/outlook-help/create-stationery-for-email-messages-HA102561327.aspx. Unique "stationery" can take an email from plain to professional. You can also include your logo and website in your custom background. Be sure to keep the background light so it will not compete with the text you will be sending.

Thank You

In this day and age it is very acceptable to send a Thank You card via email. This is an easy way to thank customers, advertisers, and even newsletter subscribers. You can create your own Thank You or use a program such as Yahoo! Greetings. Many of these programs have free e-cards as well as paid versions with additional designs. At Hallmark.com you can get free customized greeting e-cards for any occasion. An e-card is a great way to remember your clients' birthdays or perhaps a special day in their business.

Source: http://en.wikipedia.org/wiki/Email

Source: http://www.bestsyndication.com/Articles/2006/b/hart_jill/03/030306_email.htm

• | • | • | • | • | •

41. Event Registration

If you have ever attended an event and received a "goody bag" you know the power of this marketing method to reach a large number of people. Event producers enjoy providing valuable, relevant gifts to attendees as an added value. Make the most of this tactic by offering your book to event producers as part of the attendee registration package. For events with a large attendance, offer your book (up to a certain number) as an incentive to early registrants.

Why Authors Use Event Registration

Particularly if you are a speaker at the event, this tool gets your book distributed to a wider audience and also brings you increased visibility to those at the event who may be unable to attend your workshop or seminar.

THE PROCESS

•|•|•|•|•

42. Eventbrite

Eventbrite claims to be the world's fastest growing social commerce company, allowing event organizers to create an online venue for information, registration, and ticket sales. The service helps potential attendees discover your event and brings it to life.

Why Authors Use Eventbrite

Eventbrite helps you manage event activities such as registrations and ticket sales and sets you up with tools to help your event spread virally through social networks.

Source: http://www.eventbrite.com/

•|•|•|•|•

43. Ezine Articles

Expert authors and writers post their articles to be featured in numerous ezines. The searchable database of hundreds of thousands of quality original articles allows email publishers hungry for fresh content to find articles they can use for inclusion in their next newsletter.

Why Authors Write Ezine Articles

- **Free advertising** – Your author bio box is your tool to promote your own website, your book, and your personal brand and to increase visitors to your website. People who read your article will want to read more that you have written about the same topic, so be sure to direct them to more of your original content.

- **Viral marketing** – Really Simple Syndication (RSS) feeds can help you gain website traffic by submitting just one article to a directory. That same article can begin appearing on countless other websites. There are many high-visibility websites that can post your article, resulting in a flood of visitors to your site.

- **Personal and business credibility** – Publishing your articles online boosts your credibility and begins the trust cycle with your readership.

- **Traffic to your site** – Distributing your articles allows anyone to read them. This gives you an opportunity to pick up more business.

- **Sales and leads without having a site** – Even if you do not own a website, having an article online can act as your website. Make sure you complete your bio to let people know who you are. Also, include your email address so they can contact you.

Source: http://ezinearticles.com/

•|•|•|•|•

44. Facebook

Facebook is reportedly the number one social networking website. It helps you connect and share with the people in your life, past and present. Millions of people use Facebook every day to keep up with friends, upload photos, share links and videos, and learn more about the people they meet.

Why Authors Use Facebook

On Facebook you can promote your book via a personal page, a book fan page, a group, using notes or event functions, and many more ways. Your Facebook page gives fans and followers a more personal look into you, the author, and your interests.

Source: http://www.facebook.com/

• | • | • | • | •

45. fReado

fReado is the world's biggest free bookwinning site. Think of it as a giveaway site where book lovers can win free books and other prizes. These include bestselling books, rare books, and even new books and even ebook readers. To win prizes, you play a simple game, accumulate points, and use those points to bid for prizes.

Why Authors Use fReado

People love freebies. fReado is an opportunity to bring exposure to your book through giveaways.

Source: http://www.freado.com/

• | • | • | • | •

46. Gather

Gather is a site where people come together around hot topics and the things they are passionate about. Members share their expertise, advice, and views on the news of the day, and are paid for the popular content they contribute.

Why Authors Use Gather

Through Gather you can:
- Share your expertise, advice, and views on the news of the day
- Reach millions of interested readers and build your brand
- Earn money writing about what you love
- Find a variety of perspectives on topics that matter to you
- Join the conversation

Source: http://www.gather.com/

• | • | • | • | •

47. Giveaways

People love giveaways when attending events, particularly festivals, fairs, and conferences, or when frequenting retail outlets. Giveaways are, in essence, gifts that spark the curiosity of recipients and encourage them to seek more information. When people get something free it often encourages them to buy. In this way you have the opportunity to sell a higher-priced product/service and still get your book into the hands of your ideal readers. Different from contests, giveaways are offered to event attendees, members, store or site visitors, etc., not just one contest winner.

Why Authors Use Giveaways

Giving away your book might seem counterproductive to increasing sales, but when done strategically to a target group, it is an excellent way to increase visibility. When you give you also get the chance to build relationships. Providing your book or other products or services as gifts at an event—such as a book fair—draws people to your table and allows you to interact with them. To be most successful, giveaways should be done in a limited quantity for a limited time and, if possible, in exchange for the contact information of the recipients.

• | • | • | • | •

48. GoArticles

GoArticles.com is a free content article directory. When you register and upload your original articles, you are granting unconditional permission for your articles to be reprinted on other websites or print publications subject to the basic terms and conditions outlined on the site.

Why Authors Use GoArticles

By uploading your original articles, you have the opportunity to gain exposure to a wide audience through reprints of your articles. GoArticles members seek quality material for their blogs, websites, and other online publications. Any article you submit will be searchable by, and available to, visitors the day after it is submitted. The extensive online article database is updated on a regular basis.

Source: *http://goarticles.com/*

• | • | • | • | •

49. Goodreads

Launched in 2006, with over 3.4 million members who have added more than 100 million books to their shelves, Goodreads may be the largest social network for readers in the world. A place for casual readers and bonafide bookworms alike, Goodreads members recommend books, compare what they are reading, keep track of what they have read and would like to read, form book clubs, and much more.

Why Authors Join Goodreads

Goodreads is the perfect place for authors to promote their books free. It offers free access to a huge number of readers. Imagine it as a large library that readers can wander through and see everyone's bookshelves, their reviews, and their ratings. You can also post your own reviews and catalog what you have read, are currently reading, and plan to read in the future. Goodreads members can:

- Build a virtual bookshelf
- Start a group
- Sign up for Author Program
- Form a Q&A group
- Find and invite friends
- Add events
- Create a widget
- Integrate social media

Build a Virtual Bookshelf

Goodreads lets you build a shelf to display the books you have read, want to read or are reading now. Then you get to be the critic by rating and reviewing your books so your friends can see what you think.

Start a Group

Create a group around the subject of your book. You can become the resident expert in the group and talk about your books.

Signup for Author Program

The Author Program allows you to list giveaways, communicate with your fans, and syndicate your blog, book preview and video content. For example, authors can create buzz for an upcoming book by listing free copies to give away on Goodreads. You can find more at *http:// www.goodreads.com/author/program*

Form a Q&A Group

Featured Author Groups are a way for authors to interact with readers and create buzz about their books. Authors form a group and agree to answer questions about their books for a brief period, and Goodreads helps promote the group using its word-of-mouth tools.

Find and Invite Friends

Find your target market on Goodreads (i.e., avid readers) and connect with them. Search for your friends by name or email address, or send them an invitation to join Goodreads. You can also import your address book to see who is already using Goodreads.

Add Events

Publicize upcoming events, such as book signings and speaking engagements.

Create a Widget

Widgets are a way to show off what you are reading on your blog, or any other website you have. You can add the Goodreads Author widget to your personal website or blog to show off reviews of your books.

Integrate Social Media

Goodreads integrates with many other sites to allow you to show off your favorite books and easily compare books with your friends (e.g., Facebook, Twitter).

Source: http://www.goodreads.com/

• | • | • | • | • | •

50. Google+

This social networking site, owned and operated by Google, Inc., was launched in 2011. Designed primarily as a personal interaction site, Google+ allows you to organize friends and followers into "circles" for specific information sharing.

Why Authors Use Google+

As with other social media sites, Google+ allows you to interact on a personal level with friends, fans, and potential buyers. Sharing book content, information about appearances, your opinions, and related information are good ways to encourage discussion and interaction among your target audience about your book.

Source: https://plus.google.com/

• | • | • | • | • | •

51. Help A Reporter Out (HARO)

What began as a Facebook fan page in 2008 has exploded into a renowned service used by countless reporters, public relations professionals, and businesses, among others. Help A Reporter Out (HARO) is one of the fastest growing social media services in North America. Every day, HARO brings nearly 30,000 reporters and bloggers, over 100,000 news sources, and thousands of small businesses together to tell their stories, promote their brands, and sell their products and services. HARO editions go out via email at the same time every day: 5:45 am, 12:45 pm, and 5:45 pm (EST).

Why Authors Use HARO

Having firsthand knowledge of the types of stories, guests, and experts that television and radio shows seek is of tremendous value to authors who use interviews as a primary marketing strategy. Promptly and accurately responding to HARO queries that relate to your expertise and the content of your book can gain you immeasurable exposure, potential long-term visibility, and book sales.

Source: http://www.helpareporter.com/

• | • | • | • | • | •

52. Holidays

People from all walks of life celebrate holidays in various ways. These celebrations are often an opportunity for gift giving. Identify holidays related to the theme of your book. Promote the observance as a great time to give your book as a gift.

Why Authors Use Holidays

Using your book as a tie-in to a holiday or observance can boost your visibility and sales. Holidays are great limited-time-promotional opportunities. They also give you a platform to present yourself as an advocate or supporter of the concept(s) of the holiday or observance. This, in turn, could result in speaking engagements related to the topic of your book or platform.

Source: http://www.brownielocks.com/month2.html

• | • | • | • | • | •

53. HubPages

HubPages.com is an open community of writers, knowledge seekers, and conversation starters, who interact, inform, and share words, pictures, and videos. It includes a unique set of tools and resources to help "Hubbers" find and build an audience, easily create articles, and earn rewards, from accolades to ad revenue. Over 50 million people explore HubPages every month.

Why Authors Use HubPages

By contributing content to HubPages.com, you can walk others through the steps you teach in your book, start a conversation about your expertise, contribute to an existing conversation, recommend your book or business, and build followers for your website, blog, and social media community.

Source: http://www.hubpages.com

• | • | • | • | • | •

54. Joint Ventures

A joint venture takes place when two parties come together to create or enhance one project. Both parties are equally invested in the project in terms of money, time, and effort to build on the original concept. Joint ventures can help spur the success of small projects.

Why Authors Use Joint Ventures

Collaborating with others enlarges your reach to new audiences who might be potential book buyers. Forming a joint venture for which your book is a significant aspect or element of a larger project is a strategic tactic that can benefit all parties involved, including the customer.

• | • | • | • | • | •

55. Keywords

Keywords are words used by search engines to link a search to relevant web pages. Keywords can be short phrases or individual words used in your book, a title, or a business name. Keywords should be included generously within the content of your website and blog.

Why Authors Use Keywords

Keywords increase search engine optimization. Using keywords related to yourself as an author or entrepreneur, your book, or company website, blog, or other website helps people searching

THE PROCESS

online to find you.

Source: https://adwords.google.com/

• | • | • | • | • | •

56. Libraries

Libraries are most often not-for-profit organizations that house a variety of published works, from books and magazines to audio books, DVDs, and CDs. These collections are shared with patrons free of charge on a borrow/return basis. Librarians prefer to keep updated materials in stock. Therefore, they could be receptive to adding your latest book to their collections. To have your book considered for addition to a library's shelves, send a copy to the Collection Development Librarian and include a cover letter with all pertinent information about your book: summary, publication date, publisher name, genre, and ISBN.

Why Authors Use Libraries

With your book added to the shelves of your local community or school library, you could reach new readers who might not otherwise know about your book and who might then tell others about it. Libraries are great resources for getting your book reviewed by librarians, securing speaking opportunities, and simply getting your book in the hands of readers.

• | • | • | • | • | •

57. LibraryThing

An online resource and community of 1.5 million readers, LibraryThing helps people easily catalog their books. You can access your catalog from anywhere—even on your mobile phone. Because everyone catalogs together, LibraryThing also connects people with the same books and suggests what to read next.

Why Authors Use LibraryThing

Listing your book on the Authors page allows the entire LibraryThing community to know who you are. Create a personal account and include your book—and books like yours—so that other LibraryThing members can discover more about it.

Source: http://www.librarything.com/

• | • | • | • | • | •

58. Link Building

Also known as link exchange, link building is an online strategy to cross-promote websites related to your book or platform and to build exposure for your own book website. You want to have your website link appear on sites that compliment your book, business, or product and those your target audience frequents. As a trade-off, you include their links on your website.

Why Authors Use Link Building

Link Building improves search engine optimization (SEO), helping to boost your website's search engine rankings, and brings direct visits to your site so you get more traffic and sales. There is a strategy involved in link building. Wordtracker.com has a free PDF download, "Link Building Made Simple," that explains how this works. The site also features free keyword tools and training videos.

Source: http://www.wordtracker.com/

•|•|•|•|•

59. LinkedIn

When you join LinkedIn, you create a profile that summarizes your professional expertise and accomplishments. You can then form enduring connections by inviting trusted contacts to join LinkedIn and connect to you. Your network consists of your connections, your connections' connections, and the people they know, linking you to a vast number of qualified professionals and experts.

Why Authors Use LinkedIn

Linkedin provides a platform for authors to:

* Manage the information that is publicly available about you as a professional

* Find and be introduced to potential clients, service providers, and subject experts who come recommended

* Create and collaborate on projects, gather data, share files, and solve problems

* Be found for business opportunities and find potential partners

* Gain new insights from discussions with like-minded professionals in private group settings

* Discover inside connections that can help you land jobs and close deals

* Post and distribute job listings to find the best talent for your company

Source: http://www.linkedin.com/

•|•|•|•|•

60. Livestream

Livestream offers event owners a complete set of hardware and software tools to share their events with a growing online community. Founded in 2007, with Livestream more than 30 million viewers each month watch thousands of live events.

Why Authors Use Livestream

When you host live events, such as a book launch, book reading, seminar, interview, or other presentation, you give your target audience a real-time glimpse of you as the author. Sharing information about your book in a live streaming venue online is a great way to reach large numbers of people without facilities rental and other investments associated with hosting in-person-only events. During your Livestream.com event, you can even sell books and have online viewers purchase from your website.

Source: http://new.livestream.com/

• | • | • | • | • | •

61. Magazines

Periodical magazines are still a popular source of information and entertainment for millions of people. The article content is assigned to writers, either on staff or freelance. These writers are always seeking credible experts to interview and feature in their stories.

Why Authors Use Magazines

Making yourself available as a resource to article writers provides you with opportunities to be interviewed on topics related to your book subject. Additionally, many magazines feature book reviews. Submitting your book for review is best done just prior to your book's official launch, as magazines prefer to be among the first to review a book. Keep in mind that magazines often work months in advance of their publication dates. For example, the June issue of a magazine might be in production as early as January.

• | • | • | • | • | •

62. MailChimp

MailChimp is an email marketing service that allows you to design and distribute email campaigns, share them on social networks, integrate with web services you already use, manage subscribers, and track results. Use MailChimp to communicate with clients, customers, fans, buyers, and others about your activities, successes, products, programs, and services.

Why Authors Use MailChimp

Email marketing is an effective way to communicate with audiences. Using MailChimp's management systems, you can easily create professional-looking email campaigns that get the word out about your book and your brand. These campaigns allow you to promote, register, and sell to numerous people at once.

Source: http://www.mailchimp.com

• | • | • | • | • | •

63. Meetup

Meetup is the world's largest network of local groups. With more than 2,000 groups getting together in local communities every day, Meet-up makes it easy for anyone to organize a face-to-face local group or find one of thousands already meeting, each with the goal of improving themselves or their communities.

Why Authors Use Meetup

With Meetup, you can reach millions of interested readers and share your expertise, advice, and views on the news of the day. Build your brand by writing about what you love and joining the many groups and conversations.

Source: http://www.meetup.com/

• | • | • | • | •

64. MP3

MP3 is a patented encoding format for digital audio commonly used for audio storage and digital audio compression for playback on digital players. The MP3 format was designed to greatly reduce the amount of data required to represent the audio recording and still sound like a true reproduction of the original un-compressed audio.

Why Authors Use MP3

As an author, you can use this technology to record a greeting, read an excerpt, offer tips, or be interviewed about your book. You can use this recording as a free or low-cost item to sell as an accompaniment to your book or as a lead-generation tool.

• | • | • | • | •

65. Networking

Networking is simply the concept of interacting with people. As an author, you can add contacts to your network at meetings of business, social, and civic organizations as well as through online media. Groups to consider networking with include those whose members represent your ideal readers, your prospective clients or customers, and thought leaders who have influence with others.

Why Authors Use Networking

Networking is one of the best ways to get the word out about your book. Authors can distribute business cards and other information about their books at networking events. Some networking events allow attendees to display products, such as books, and to introduce themselves to the entire group. This provides you "face time" with decision makers, book buyers, those who schedule speakers for other meetings and events, and prospective clients or customers.

• | • | • | • | •

66. Newsletters

A newsletter is a regularly distributed publication generally about one main topic that is of interest to its subscribers. Newspapers and leaflets are types of newsletters. Additionally, newsletters delivered electronically via email (eNewsletters) have gained rapid acceptance for the same reasons email in general has gained popularity over printed correspondence.

Why Authors Use Newsletters

Newsletters provide access to potential readers with specific interests in the topic of your book.

THE PROCESS

Send an announcement to organizations to which you belong and let them know you are an author. Ask if they can include an announcement about your book in their next issue.

Popular newsletter sources include:
- Communities
- Churches
- Associations
- Alumni
- Colleges
- Ministries
- Fraternities and Sororities

• | • | • | • | • | •

67. Newspapers

A newspaper is a regularly scheduled publication containing news, information, and advertising. With the dawn of the Internet, newspapers have had to compete with online media. With online newspapers, many of the forms of printed advertising are now free on newspaper websites.

Why Authors Use Newspapers

As an author you can do the following with a newspaper:
- Post an online event
- Add a venue
- Add a performance
- Post classifieds
- Submit event listings
- Send news tips
- Submit editorials
- Write book reviews
- Write articles
- Write for a column

• | • | • | • | • | •

68. Nonprofit/Not-for-Profit Organizations

Groups that exist to serve others or provide information or support that are not federally taxed and use surplus revenues to achieve their goals rather than distributing them as profit or dividends are considered nonprofit organizations. Often these groups include a base of members, clients, or supporters who respect and connect with the organization regularly. There are tens of thousands of nonprofit/not-for-profit organizations in the United States and around the world.

Why Authors Use Nonprofit/Not-for-Profit Organizations

Connecting with nonprofit/not-for-profit organizations whose charters or interests fall in line with your book is a key strategy for building relationships, credibility, and visibility for your book and for you as an author. By forming a formal or informal relationship with such groups you can sell books to the group at a reduced rate and suggest they offer your book as part of their membership renewal incentive, as a thank-you gift for donors, or as gifts for their board of directors.

Source: http://www.idealist.org/info/Nonprofits

• | • | • | • | •

69. NothingBinding

Specially designed for writers, authors, readers, and book buyers, NothingBinding.com is a launch site for writers. It unites these groups around the world. NothingBinding gives undiscovered and rising writers and authors a unique platform to showcase their works to readers and book buyers.

Why Authors Use NothingBinding

When you join NothingBinding, you can promote your books and connect with fellow writers, authors, readers, and book buyers.

Source: http://www.nothingbinding.com/

• | • | • | • | •

70. Partnerships

A partnership is an intentional collaborative effort between two or more parties that have a common goal and a common audience. These efforts might include packaging books and information products, or collaborating on live or online events. Each partner essentially provides a third party endorsement of the other.

Why Authors Use Partnerships

Partnerships provide opportunities to share the information in your book with a broader audience, thereby enhancing your exposure. Additionally, you can engage directly with readers you might not otherwise reach by accessing the loyal audience of your partner(s).

• | • | • | • | •

71. Patch

Patch is an information and engagement platform for community specific news, allowing neighbors to connect with one other, their communities, and the national conversation. Content is user driven, meaning that authors and others can submit announcements, press releases, photographs, and other information to be viewed by readers.

Why Authors Use Patch

With Patch, you can get out the word about your book, your business, and your brand to many communities. This is an effective platform to gain visibility for a book launch or event, to

THE PROCESS

position yourself as an expert, or to provide information and tips that support the content and theme of your book.

Source: http://www.patch.com/

• | • | • | • | •

72. Pinterest

Pinterest lets you organize and share all the beautiful things you find on the web. People use pin-boards to plan their weddings, decorate their homes, and organize their favorite recipes. Best of all, you can browse pin-boards created by other people. Browsing pin-boards is a fun way to discover new things and get inspiration from people who share your interests.

Why Authors Use Pinterest

As an author, you can be promote your book in many ways using Pinterest. From your Pinterest page you can create different boards for different interests related to your book. For example, you can create a board for your book cover(s), one showing the characters in your book, one for behind the scenes pictures of you while writing the book, and one for you interacting with your readers, etc. In addition, other people can pin things to your board to encourage more sharing and interaction. Here are the benefits to use as an author:

- **Tell your story** - Show what you are about with rich visuals

- **Build a community** - Get to know other pinners who follow you

- **Send traffic your way** - Make it easy for people to find and share your stuff

- **Learn and grow** - See what is working well and how to get better

Source: http://pinterest.com/

• | • | • | • | •

73. Podcasts

A podcast is an audio recording that can be downloaded and shared. You might create a podcast of you discussing your book, reading an excerpt, or being interviewed by someone about the content or process of writing the book.

Why Authors Use Podcasts

You can use podcasts to encourage customers to buy your book by sharing tips, reading excerpts, discussing your writing process, or providing information about how readers can benefit from your book content.

Source: To upload your podcast to the Apple iTunes store, visit http://www.apple.com/itunes/podcasts/creatorfaq.html

• | • | • | • | •

74. Portable Document Format (PDF)

PDF is an electronic file format designed to allow users to view and transmit documents regardless of application software, hardware, and operating systems. It allows you to create documents to be shared via email and website upload.

Why Authors Use PDF

As an author, you can turn portions or excerpts of your book into PDF files for your website or blog. These giveaways could encourage ezine or RSS feed subscribers to buy your book, or could be used as handouts at speaking engagements.

Source: http://www.adobe.com

• | • | • | • | •

75. Press Releases

Press releases—also called news releases, media releases, or press statements—are written or recorded communications directed at members of the news media for the purpose of making purportedly newsworthy announcements. Typically, they are e-mailed to assignment editors at newspapers, magazines, radio stations, television stations, and/or television networks.

Why Authors Use Press Releases

Writing and distributing a press release is an effective way to reach journalists and other targeted groups about your book, thereby providing them with information to share with their audiences who could then purchase your book. Use press releases to announce the initial launch of your book or to mention awards, accolades, appearances, and other timely news tie-ins. Your press release should include your book title, your name and contact information, a summary of your book, a brief quote from you about why you wrote the book, a comment about your book from a reviewer or industry expert, the book's ISBN, your website, and where the book can be purchased.

• | • | • | • | •

76. Pubmatch

If you want your book to be the next best seller, PubMatch is the ideal place for you. This is where international publishers, publicists, literary agents, and agencies search for talent. At PubMatch, authors can create a profile and add their book titles, which enters them into the searchable database.

Why Authors Use Pubmatch

Pubmatch provides advanced author search techniques to facilitate building relationships with other authors and industry experts around the world. It provides a huge platform where you can share your manuscripts and other data.

Source: http://www.pubmatch.org/

• | • | • | • | •

THE PROCESS

77. Radio Interviews

There are thousands of radio stations in the United States, and thousands more on the Internet and through satellite radio. Many radio stations host news and information programs where experts and authors engage in discussions, often by telephone, about topics of interest to listeners. Radio interviews provide authors opportunities to share their knowledge and information about their book by allowing listeners to call in to the programs to ask questions.

Why Authors Use Radio Interviews

Readers connect with authors over a message. When readers hear your interview on the radio you have the opportunity to connect with their emotions. You position yourself as an expert and share concepts from your book. This then incites listeners to purchase your book and to tell others about you. To make radio interviews most successful:

- Listen to the program before you go on as a guest
- Prepare talking points related to your expertise and the content of your book
- Know the focus of the interview
- Maintain contact with the host and producer before and after your appearance

Source: http://www.radiopublicity.com

• | • | • | • | •

78. Radio Guest List

Thousands of broadcast programs are seeking qualified, interesting, entertaining experts and personalities to feature on their shows, including podcasts, talk radio, Internet and satellite radio, and TV. Radio Guest List delivers a daily listing of such shows right to your email in-box. The listings include the program and host name, type of media, description of the types of guests being sought, and contact information.

Why Authors Use Radio Guest List

Getting booked for interviews on radio and TV is one of the best ways to expand your visibility. The programs listed on Radio Guest List offer opportunities to share with audiences the content and concepts in your book, as well as to promote related products, services, and events.

Source: http://www.radioguestlist.com/

• | • | • | • | •

79. ReadersCircle

ReadersCircle is a site that allows readers to start or join book clubs where people discuss whatever they are reading. Sometimes participants decide to discuss an "optional book." Otherwise, people just bring their own books, articles, and magazines, and the conversation goes from there. The idea is to loosen the usual book club format so participants can select their own reading and attend even if they are still in the middle of the book. Conversations inevitably cover the books brought and many other subjects as well.

Why Authors Use ReadersCircle
Reader's circles offer an ideal way to gain exposure to a broad market and to sell multiple books. As an author, you can contact local book clubs to visit their meetings and engage in conversations about your book. Becoming a *Virtual Author* where you participate over the phone or the Internet will expand the number of book clubs in which you can participate.

Source: http://www.readerscircle.org/

• | • | • | • | •

80. RedRoom

RedRoom is an online bookstore that shares profits with authors and connects readers and authors online. The online community includes thousands of aspiring and published authors—famous and almost discovered—professional journalists, and publishing professionals including editors, agents, booksellers, librarians, and seriously devoted readers. You can create a profile and add book titles, audio, video, blog posts, and more.

Why Authors Use RedRoom
As with other social media sites, RedRoom.com is an interactive forum for connecting readers, writers, and the overall literary community. As an author, you can write a blog and watch your RedRoom dashboard to see how many people are reading it. RedRoom also offers an opportunity for you to sell your books and receive greater royalties than on many other online bookstores.

Source: http://redroom.com/

• | • | • | • | •

81. Reporter Connection

Reporter Connection is a free daily email service that connects journalists with experts available for media interviews. Established in 1985, the parent company of Reporter Connection, Bradley Communications Corp., has been connecting journalists and sources for over 24 years. The company is best known for publishing "RadioTV Interview Report" (RTIR), the twice-monthly magazine that 4,000 radio/TV producers across the United States read to find interesting guests, as well as hosting the National Publicity Summit, a conference at which attendees have the opportunity to learn from and personally meet top journalists and producers.

Why Authors Use Reporter Connection
Reporter Connection helps you find reporters and producers who are actively looking for sources on your particular subject. Join as an expert/source and receive the free daily media opportunities. When you see a listing to which you wish to respond, click the link to be connected to that listing on the website. Answer the journalist's questions and provide your contact information. Your response is immediately e-mailed to the journalist. If interested, the journalist will get in touch with you directly.

Source: http://www.reporterconnection.com/

THE PROCESS

• | • | • | • | •

82. Repurposing

Repurposing refers to extracting portions of your book for use in blogs, social media posts, information products, scripts for teleseminars, speeches, PowerPoint presentations, and the like. Repurposing allows you to get your message out in various ways and to position you as an expert and a seasoned author.

Why Authors Use Repurposing

One of the easiest ways to get more "mileage" from your book's content, with a little creativity, you can find many uses for repurposing the content you have already created in your book. This provides another stream of revenue, to capture leads, or to promote your platform.

• | • | • | • | •

83. Scribd

Scribd is considered the world's largest online library. The platform makes it easy to share and discover entertaining, informative, and original written content across the Web and mobile devices. Scribd's platform is designed to help you easily publish your content on the Web and mobile devices, distribute it to a wide and global audience, and potentially make money from selling that content.

Why Authors Use Scribd

By publishing on Scribd, you can publish portions of your book or your entire content which can be seen by up to 90 million people from all around the world who use Scribd. Scribd instantly turns documents into formatted web pages and does SEO for you so that every word of your content is fully indexed by all major search engines. Scribd socially optimizes all content to maximize social distribution. If you choose to, you can set a price for your content and make it for sale through a simple link, and the earnings go right to your account.

Source: http://www.scribd.com/

• | • | • | • | •

84. Shelfari

Shelfari is a social network for people who love books. Shelfari introduces readers to a global community of book lovers and encourages them to share their literary inclinations and passions with peers, friends, and total strangers. Shelfari is a gathering place for authors, aspiring authors, publishers, and readers, and has many tools and features to help these groups connect in a fun and engaging way. Its mission is to enhance the experience of reading by connecting readers in meaningful conversations about the published word. Shelfari was officially launched in October 2006 and was acquired by Amazon.com in August 2008.

Why Authors Use Shelfari

With Shelfari, you can find your target market and connect with them. You can create a virtual shelf to show off your book, see what your friends are reading, and discover new books. It lets you display what you have read and what you want to read. You get to be a critic, rating and reviewing books so your friends can see what you think. See which books you have in common with others. Ask your friends for book recommendations and recommend your book to them. Shelfari also has a widget you can add to your blog or social networking site. You can create a group around the subject of your book, become the resident expert, and talk about your book. Search for your friends by name or email address, or send them an invitation to join Shelfari. You can also import your address book to see who is already using Shelfari.

Source: http://www.shelfari.com/

• | • | • | • | •

85. Signature "Sig" Files

A signature file is a brief message or contact information displayed at the bottom of all your outgoing emails. It can be created in your email settings and can include book ordering information, a quote from your book, upcoming book signing dates, or a link to your website or blog, or whatever you wish.

Why Authors Use Signature Files

Every method of communication is an opportunity to promote your book, including the emails you send on a daily basis. Signature files provide an easy and concise way to consistently share information and direct your contacts to key web pages and book information. Change your signature file from time to time to promote news related to your book.

• | • | • | • | •

86. Slideshare

SlideShare is a business media site for sharing presentations, documents, and PDFs. SlideShare features a vibrant professional community that regularly comments, "favorites," and downloads content. Content also spreads virally through blogs and social networks such as LinkedIn, Facebook, and Twitter. Individuals and organizations upload documents to SlideShare to share ideas, connect with others, and generate leads for their businesses. Anyone can view presentations and documents on topics that interest them.

Why Authors Use SlideShare

SlideShare is an ideal way to get your slides on the Web so your ideas can be found and shared by a wide audience. With features available on SlideShare you can:

- Embed slideshows into your own blog or website
- Share slideshows publicly or privately
- Synch audio to your slides
- Market your own event

THE PROCESS

- Join groups to connect with other SlideShare members who share your interests

Source: http://www.slideshare.net/

• | • | • | • | •

87. Speaking

Although public speaking is feared by many, it is almost a necessity for successful authors. Being able to share the information in your book and the process of writing and publishing it could provide a wellspring of sales and visibility opportunities. Creating a signature talk or standard presentation related to your book is essential in capturing the attention of audiences and communicating the main points included in your book. Many organizations and coaches are available to provide assistance in perfecting presentation skills and teaching you how to sell before, during, and after your presentation.

Why Authors Use Speaking

Giving presentations about your book to organizations, clubs, groups, conferences, schools, churches, libraries, and other gatherings where your target audience can be found is a prime opportunity to promote your platform and sell your book. Whether or not you receive payment for speaking, being able to sell your book at the venue after your presentation—known as "back of the room sales"—is crucial. Equally beneficial is the opportunity to schedule additional speaking engagements and appearances through those in the audience who know of other groups that could benefit from your expertise.

88. Suite101

Suite101 is a new kind of knowledgebase centered on personal experience and passionate interest. They bring together people who thrive on sharing what they have been through, what they know, what they care about.

The website is more focused than a forum, more dynamic than an encyclopedia, Suite101 is all about weaving real experiences into knowledge. On Suite101, your interests determine the structure and every contribution is an opportunity to connect with a personal, guided entry point into any subject.

The goal of Suite101 is to help build a freer, more cooperative internet by creating an environment that encourages the exchange of ideas.

Why Authors Use Suite101

Suite101 enables authors to connect with their target audience by sharing a personal experience(s). Authors can:

- Share their passions to give readers a glimpse into the world of writing from the eyes of the author
- Discover more about their target audience through a dialogue
- Connect with others that share a common interest

Source: http://suite101.com/

• | • | • | • | •

89. Teach a Course/Seminar/Workshop

Your book can be used as content for a course, seminar, or workshop that you can teach. Colleges, universities, conferences, camps, and other academic venues are excellent outlets to share your book's content.

Why Authors Use Teaching

Teaching the content of your book to others further positions you as an expert and establishes you as the "go-to" person for answers on the subject about which you have written. Teaching also helps perfect your presentation skills and places you in an academic forum, providing exposure to a community of broad thinkers and influencers within the higher learning arena.

• | • | • | • | •

90. Teleseminars/Teleclasses

Akin to in-person seminars, teleseminars and teleclasses are learning sessions you host and conduct via telephone conferencing. There are a number of ways to format your teleseminar. You can teach sections of your book yourself, invite experts to share their insights on topics related to your book, interview other experts, or even have someone interview you. Overall, teleseminars should be designed to teach listeners a concept.

Why Authors Use Teleseminars/Teleclasses

Though usually offered free of charge, teleseminars "seed" participants to purchase products, services, or programs you offer alone or through a partnership or joint venture. For your teleseminar, select a topic related to your book's content, invite a few experts to participate, invite others to listen and ask questions, and make an offer at the end.

• | • | • | • | •

91. Testimonials

When someone says or writes something great about you or your book, that is called a testimonial. You can get testimonials by asking readers to share their positive thoughts about your book. They can be posted on your website or blog, included in your marketing materials, or read during an interview or speech.

Why Authors Use Testimonials

Testimonials help others know that someone has already had a positive experience or result from reading your book, and the comments encourage others to want to buy your book. Testimonials are considered "third-party endorsements" or "peer endorsements" and are highly influential to potential buyers.

• | • | • | • | •

THE PROCESS

92. Trade Associations

Nearly every industry has an association that represents its members, lobbies to protect its interests, and provides information to the general public. Most often, members of the trade association are companies or organizations that have a common bond. These groups meet regularly to share information about enhancing their individual companies/organizations and improving the visibility and image of their entire industry.

Why Authors Use Trade Associations

Connecting with trade associations can help build visibility for your book and awareness of your brand and your platform. You could present yourself as a speaker for annual conventions, professional development sessions, webinars, and other meetings and events. Additionally, as appropriate, you could offer your book as a training manual or industry guide. This could further establish you as an expert and promote you as a knowledgeable author.

• | • | • | • | •

93. Twitter

Twitter is a real-time information network powered by people all around the world that lets them share and discover what is happening immediately with people and organizations they care about.

Why Authors Use Twitter

As an author, through tweets (micro posts) you can keep interested readers updated in a casual manner.

Source: http://twitter.com/

• | • | • | • | •

94. Videos

Sharing videos is a popular and highly influential way to market your book, business, product, or service. Use the webcam on your computer, a Flipcam, or even the video feature on your smartphone to record your video. Once you have created your video, upload it to your website or a free video hosting site. Videos do not have to be high in production quality. However, the sound and lighting should be effective to enhance the viewing experience. Here are a few areas you could cover with a video:

- Talk about the content of your book
- Describe the process of writing the book
- Read an excerpt
- Explain who the book is for/who should read it
- Describe what readers can get out of your book
- Offer a special price or package
- Mention an event (book signing, speaking engagement, seminar) where you will be

- Describe your book's characters
- Explain why you wrote the book
- Explain how to use the book
- Highlight a case study or example included in the book
- Have someone interview you about the book

Why Authors Use Videos

Video sharing can increase book sales by allowing you to share information about your book and have viewers get to know you as the author. To help make your video most effective, include an offer and call to action, such as, "Visit our website to order ..." Explain how purchasing the book or other products and services is easy. Walk viewers through the steps.

• | • | • | • | •

95. Vimeo

Vimeo is a social network for sharing information via video. In 2004, a group of filmmakers founded it to share their creative work and personal moments from their lives. Today, millions of people upload personal, business, and instructional videos to Vimeo for sharing around the world.

Why Authors Use Vimeo

You can use Vimeo to share videos about your book or use content from it as a script that will inform, inspire, teach, and entertain. Include book pricing, contact information, and links to your website and other social media sites so potential buyers can purchase your book and spread the word to their friends and colleagues.

Source: http://www.vimeo.com

• | • | • | • | •

96. Virtual Book Tours

Virtual book tours allow you to promote your book while interacting with various bloggers and online media outlets. Similar to in-person book tours, virtual book tours occur over a set period of time and include visits, stops, or appearances on various online venues. These could include live webinars, posting on popular blogs and article sites, podcasts, video interviews, and more. They could also include write-ups or original content you post about your book that appear during the tour dates. Hosting a successful virtual book tour takes effective scheduling, solid relationships with online venues, tracking mechanisms to respond to comments/posts, and visible promotion to ensure your audience of potential readers follows the tour and ultimately buys your book.

Why Authors Use Virtual Book Tours

If your target audience is active online conducting a virtual book tour allows you to connect with them in a convenient venue—neither they nor you have to travel—and share information so they will immediately buy your book. Virtual book tours allow instant interaction and feedback with audiences, as well as broad word of mouth appeal across various online platforms.

Source: http://bit.ly/RNrsxM

• | • | • | • | • | •

97. Webinars/Webcasts

Short for web-based seminar, a webinar is a presentation, lecture, workshop or seminar that is transmitted over the Web. Webinars offer interactive elements: the ability to give, receive, and discuss information whereas webcasts offer only one-way data transmission and do not include interaction between the presenter and the audience.

Why Authors Use Webinars/Webcasts

Webinars and webcasts help you increase your credibility, enhancing your reputation, showing what you know via educational events related to your book. Demonstrating your knowledge and expertise will build your business, drawing traffic to your website or blog, and causing readers to become clients. In addition, webinars allow you to respond to attendees' questions and comments.

• | • | • | • | • | •

98. Wikispaces

Wikis are web pages that groups, friends, and families can edit together. Starting your wiki at Wikispaces is fast, free, and easy.

Why Authors Use Wikispaces

With Wikispaces you can easily collaborate with others. Using its invitation system, you can invite people to your wiki and begin collaborating right away. You can also participate in discussion forums to further enhance your online relationships and following.

Source: http://www.wikispaces.com/

99. Word of Mouth

One of the oldest and most effective forms of marketing, word of mouth is people telling others about their experiences using your products or services, including your book. Ideally, the comments are positive and happen naturally. As people read your book they wish to tell others about it. Many authors encourage word-of-mouth marketing by asking readers to comment about their book on social networks. In essence, positive word-of-mouth marketing is viewed by others as third party endorsements, much like testimonials.

Why Authors Use Word of Mouth

Word-of-mouth marketing can benefit you as an author in the following ways:

- **Buzz Marketing** – Using high profile entertainment or news to get people to talk about your brand

- **Viral Marketing** – Creating entertaining or informative messages designed to be passed along in an exponential fashion, often electronically or by email

- **Community Marketing** – Forming or supporting niche communities that are likely to share interests about your brand (such as user groups, fan clubs, and discussion forums) and providing tools, content, and information to support those communities

- **Grassroots Marketing** – Organizing and motivating volunteers to engage in personal or local outreach

- **Evangelist Marketing** – Cultivating evangelists, advocates, or volunteers who are encouraged to take a leadership role in actively spreading the word on your behalf

- **Product Seeding** – Placing the right product into the right hands at the right time, providing information or samples to influential individuals

- **Influencer Marketing** – Identifying key communities and opinion leaders who are likely to talk about products and have the ability to influence the opinions of others

- **Cause Marketing** – Supporting social causes to earn respect and support from people who feel strongly about the cause

- **Conversation Creation** – Interesting or fun advertising, emails, catchphrases, entertainment, or promotions designed to start wordofmouth activity

- **Brand Blogging** – Creating blogs and participating in the blogosphere in the spirit of open, transparent communication by sharing information of value that the blog community may talk about

- **Referral Programs** – Creating tools that enable satisfied customers to refer their friends

Source: © 2005 Word of Mouth Marketing Association; Word of Mouth 101, An Introduction to Word of Mouth Marketing

• | • | • | • | •

100. WordPress

WordPress is an open source system for hosting your blog. Featuring hundreds of themed templates, WordPress includes social media links (Facebook, Twitter, LinkedIn, and more), statistics to track your blog readers, mobile apps for various mobile platforms, a multilingual dashboard, online support, and other tools.

Why Authors Use WordPress

A WordPress blog allows you to easily create a blog to share information about your book, comment about topics related to your industry or interests, and build an online following, further building your credibility and increasing your book sales.

Source: http://www.wordpress.com

THE PROCESS

Source: http://wordpress.org/

• | • | • | • | • | •

101. YouTube

Founded in February 2005, YouTube is the world's most popular online video community, allowing millions of people to discover, watch, and share originally-created videos.

Why Authors Use YouTube

With the YouTube forum you can connect with, inform, and inspire others across the globe. It acts as a distribution platform for original content creators and advertisers, large and small. Videos you post to YouTube can be used to promote your book, your business, or your brand, provide informative tips about your area of expertise, announce product sales, speaking engagements, or read excerpts from your book.

Source: http://www.youtube.com/

APPENDICES

21 Tips to Prepare for a Book Signing

As professionals in the publishing industry, we are saddened by how little effort some authors put into publicizing and promoting their book signings. There can be several reasons, but one is most often true—they do not know how. Listed below are 21 techniques for preparing for a book signing. Implementing these techniques will enhance results.

1. Email: Email all your contacts to let them know you will participate in a book signing. Provide them with details about the event and encourage them to support you with their attendance. Ask them to forward your email to at least 10 friends. Within minutes, you could reach thousands of people.

2. Newsletter: Send an announcement to organizations to which you belong (e.g., church, community, school, alumni association, sorority, fraternity, etc.) and let them know you will participate in a book signing. Ask if they can include the announcement in their next communication.

3. Facebook Friends: Create an EVENT on Facebook and invite all your Facebook friends. Ask them to SHARE the event with their Facebook friends.

4. Facebook Networks: Send an email to your Facebook Networks and ask the FAN page owner to announce your participation in a book signing. Also, ask them to enter the book signing as an EVENT on their FAN page.

5. Facebook Page: Create a Facebook Page for you as an author and SUGGEST the page to your Facebook friends.

6. Twitter: Tweet... Tweet... Tweet... about your book signing and ask your followers to retweet.

7. Website: Add the book signing to your website and encourage visitors to attend.

8. Promotional Materials: Bring promotional materials to support your book, such as banners, posters, bookmarks, postcards, business cards, flyers, etc., to the book signing. Make sure your materials look professional, clear, and concise.

9. Interaction: Plan activities at your book signing such as author readings, trivia contests, giveaways, or mini-workshops. Pass out candy, bookmarks, and stickers. Display a schedule of events so people will be informed. Consider an offer of a gift with purchase (e.g., a coloring page based on your children's book with a small box of crayons).

10. Decorate: Create an atmosphere that is warm and inviting. Decorate the book signing area with items such as tablecloths, plants, beanbags, artwork, music, etc. Provide space for attendees to sit and read your book.

APPENDICES

11. Book Display: Make your book display fun and inviting. For example, if you have a cookbook, wrap a spoon, fork, napkin, and plate around it with raffia or create a basket with fun items related to your book.

12. Dress: Dress the part so people will have a visual of the main parts of your book. If your book is about a princess, wear a tiara and a pretty dress.

13. Mailing List: Create a form for attendees to sign up for your mailing list so you can communicate with them after the book signing. Be sure to write immediately to thank them for stopping by and inform them of your future events. Say "thank you" if they purchased your book.

14. Network: Prepare your 30-second "elevator speech." Book signings are attended by a variety of people (literary agents, publishers, booksellers, librarians, educators, and more), so network with as many people as you can. Do not look at the book signing as a competition with the other authors. Instead, make it a time to celebrate books and all who love to write and read. Ask everyone a prepared question to break the ice. "Are you a writer?" "What do you like most about book signings?" "What other book signings have you attended?" Look for ways to share your "elevator speech."

15. Exposure: Develop a plan to get exposure. For example, tell attendees an unforgettable vignette about you or share a story behind the story (i.e., your book) that is intriguing and will be remembered. Book sales are not guaranteed at a book signing, but you can make a lasting impression that could lead to future sales. Remember, book lovers can purchase your book on the Internet 24/7, so leave an unforgettable impression.

16. Price: Price your book in whole dollars and bring lots of change in appropriate denominations. For example, if your book retails for $15.95, round up to $16.00. Also, provide purchasers a bag containing your other promotional materials. Offer to include other author's promotional materials in your bag if they will do the same for you.

17. Signs: Bring a sign that says "Autographed Copies" because people love autographed books from known and unknown authors. Also, hang a sign that will appeal to your target market, such as "Perfect Gift for Teens/Dads/Moms/Grandparents/Christmas," etc.

18. Audience: Create <u>YOUR</u> own stage. Set out a few chairs in your assigned area. If you are a children's book author, bring puppets of characters from your book and have a puppet show.

19. Buttons: Wear a button or pin that promotes your book or a generic one, such as "Ask Me," to grab the attention of browsers. This opens lines of communication so you can give your sales pitch.

20. Balance: Find the right balance between selling and overselling. Invite attendees to buy by creating an atmosphere that is comfortable and non-threatening. If you are pushy, you may push them away and lose them as customers.

21. Media: Set up radio, TV, or newspaper interviews prior to the book signing to create awareness. For example, contact the producer of a local radio show. Pitch your story, NOT your book. Producers and newspaper editorial writers want to hear a personal story about you and the reason for the book. (Note: Each radio show has a different producer; likewise for TV.)

APPENDICES

Book Festival Tips

The energy at book festivals and fairs can be electric with the people, the entertainment, the booths, the food, and more. Book events, however, can be taxing for an author. Whether a book signing or book festival, it can sometimes be difficult to get the most out of the event if you do not go into it with a clear strategy and expectations. What do you want to accomplish? Do you know the audience that will be at the event? What is the overall cost to you? How will you measure your success? Unfortunately, many authors do not consider these questions when they commit to doing book events. They think they will simply show up, spread their table linens, set out a few books, and sell, sell, sell. Actually, it does not work that way.

You must have a strategy for any appearance you make, whether a speaking engagement, a media interview, a book signing, or a book fair. Over the years, we have coordinated book festivals and dozens of appearances for authors, companies, and organizations, and we know what it takes to leverage your investment of time and money while onsite. Here are a few tips to help make your book festival experience enjoyable and effective.

Count the cost: Determine how much the event will cost you in booth rental, linens, signage, product (books), giveaways, and most importantly, time.

Help me out: Be sure you will have some help while onsite. Depending on the size of the crowd, one person might be plenty, but in some instances you will need two or three others to help answer questions about your book, take payments, and more. Be sure your assistants are well acquainted with you, your book, and your platform.

Speaking of your platform: Your appearance should be an opportunity to enhance, expand, or increase the visibility of your platform. You want to sell books, of course, but you should also be prepared to share about your bigger vision, whether that is your business or your cause.

Make the rounds: Arrive early, set up your table, leave your trusty assistant there, and visit the other booths. Introduce yourself, pick up their business cards, and be cordial. You never know who might be a good partner, referral source, or customer.

Stand up and stand out: Get off your tush! Please do not sit the entire time. Stand up and greet people as they walk by, especially when they walk up to your booth. Nothing says, "Please don't bother me," like someone sitting behind a table.

Grab them: Not literally, but come up with a short, catchy phrase or question to grab the attention of people walking by.

Collect leads: Many authors hand out bookmarks, postcards, and business cards at their tables, but few actually collect leads. This is one of the primary reasons for attending fairs and festivals. You want to be able to follow up with those who visit your table. Send a follow-up email to thank them for stopping by your table, add them to your ezine subscribers list, invite them to follow your blog, visit your website, or attend your next speaking engagement. Maximize each and every contact.

Measure success: Before you even arrive, decide how you are going to measure the success of the event ... and please do not let it be by book sales alone. Consider how many leads you want to collect, important connections you want to make, booth and signage positioning for visibility, media opportunities.

Trade shows, book fairs, and festivals are not for the weak-hearted author. Personal appearances require focus, determination, strategy, and stamina. So next time you sign up to participate in an event to promote your book keep the above tips in mind.

APPENDICES

American Library Association Awards

The American Library Association (ALA) Awards Program annually awards recipients for outstanding service to the profession. This program provides continuing education through scholarships, grants for future projects, and awards for distinguished service. It is the intent that all award winners share their achievement by nominating colleagues or individuals for an award. For a list of book awards published by the American Library Association (ALA), visit http://www.ala.org/awardsgrants/awards/browse/bpma?showfilter=no

About the Authors

Nicole Antoinette

Nicole Antoinette is an information technology specialist, author, independent business consultant, adjunct college professor, and publisher.

After leading large teams in corporate America for 17 years, Nicole launched Faith Books & MORE in June 2008 by faith as promised in her life verse: "I will instruct you and teach you in the way you should go; I will counsel you and watch over you" (Psalm 32:8). She believes writers have an obligation to preserve their thoughts, experiences, creativity, and most importantly, their faith in print as well as through other forms of media.

Nicole is a results-driven professional with multi-faceted technology experience leading large implementation engagements. With strong leadership qualifications in management and planning, developing processes, building high-performance teams, and managing innovation, she has worked directly with and presented to C-level executive leadership. Nicole is recognized as a perceptive leader with demonstrated ability to lead a diverse team of professionals. She has 20 years of experience in Executive Leadership, Process Improvement, Project Management, Program Management, Software Quality Assurance, and Business Analysis with in-depth working knowledge and hands-on experience in Software Development Life Cycle, Software Quality Assurance methodologies and tools, managing SaaS, Clouding Computing, and eCommerce projects.

Nicole earned her Master of Science degree in Computer Information Systems from Missouri State University and her Bachelor of Business Administration degree (with majors in both Management Information Systems and Marketing) while playing basketball on a scholarship at Ohio University.

APPENDICES

Anita Rochelle

Anita Rochelle Paul is a communications specialist, known as "The Author's Midwife." She coaches and mentors corporate professionals and successful entrepreneurs to become published authors. Through her Write Your Life program, she shares strategies for writing, publishing, and marketing a book.

A 20-year veteran of the marketing communications industry, Anita started The Write Image in 1997. A corporate communications company, The Write Image develops marketing and public relations programs for mid-sized businesses, nonprofit organizations, and trade associations. She uses her extensive planning, organizing, and strategic marketing skills to help clients develop effective communications strategies and public relations campaigns throughout the United States.

After years of working with decision-makers in various industries she realized many were "secret agents"—super intelligent, well-respected, knowledgeable leaders who were experts in their fields, yet nobody knew it. She wondered what would help these experts get noticed. The answer: Every expert needs a book of his/her own. So she developed a program to help professionals upsell their expertise. "Women (and men) in business need a calling card, a defining brand, a product to demonstrate their knowledge and their expertise," says Anita. "A well-written book is one of the best tools to brand professionals as experts in their field so they can gain the visibility, recognition, and opportunities to take their careers and their businesses to a higher level and to earn more money." Her passion for mentoring authors to overcome obstacles to their publishing success became her focus, and thus, "Write Your Life" was created.

Designed to reinforce a business platform for existing authors, and to establish and support a budding brand for aspiring authors, Write Your Life is a unique, comprehensive program for establishing your expertise and leveraging your book as part of your brand. "It's bigger than the book," says Anita. "You have an idea, a business objective, a career goal, a brand, or a grand vision. We work to create a book that will support that platform, brand you as an expert, and get you going in the right direction." As an author and freelance writer, Anita has authored and co-authored several books and articles for over 25 trade publications in the U.S. and Canada. She speaks to and instructs audiences on various topics related to writing and independent book publishing. She hosts the show, "Book Your Success."

Other Books by Nicole Antoinette

Box of Chocolates
ISBN: 978-0-9860247-5-7

Box of Chocolates for Teens
ISBN: 978-0-9860247-6-4

Building Blocks for Effective Software Testing
ISBN: 978-0-9820197-1-9

Getting Beyond the Day™ - Your Guide to Surviving a Job Layoff
ISBN: 978-0-9860159-2-2

Getting Beyond the Day™ - Your Guide to Surviving a Job Layoff Workbook
ISBN: 978-0-9860159-6-0

Getting Beyond the Day™ Journal
ISBN: 978-1-939761-05-7

Strategic Life Planning for Single Parents
ISBN: 978-0-9860247-9-5

The Executive's Guide to Cost Optimization
ISBN: 978-0-9820197-3-3

Other Books by Anita Rochelle

Write Your Life: Create Your Ideal Life and the Book You've Been Wanting to Write
ISBN: 978-1-61005-062-3

Publishing as a Marketing Strategy
ISBN: 978-1-61005-114-9

Book Your Success: Write Your Book in 90 Days or Less
A self-study program